THE LITTLE

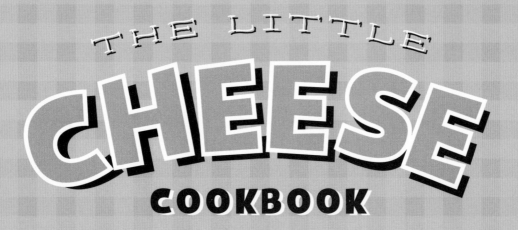

CHEESE

COOKBOOK

LAURA HERRING

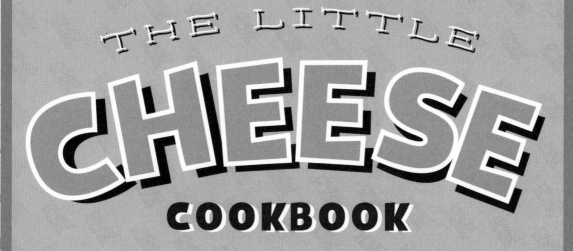

THE LITTLE CHEESE COOKBOOK

FROM SNACKS TO SWEETS —
BECAUSE CHEESE GOES WITH EVERYTHING!

Smith
Street
Books

CONTENTS

INTRODUCTION

WHAT CAN'T BE IMPROVED WITH EXTRA CHEESE? WHAT IS A BOWL OF PASTA WITHOUT A HEAVY SNOWDRIFT OF PARMESAN? A PIZZA *NEEDS* A STRINGY MESS OF MOZZARELLA ON TOP. AND IS THERE ANYTHING MORE SATISFYING, COMFORTING AND MIND-BLOWINGLY MOREISH IN THIS WORLD THAN AN OOZING, MOLTEN CHEESE TOASTIE? I THINK PROBABLY NOT. EVEN A BAD DAY IS INFINITELY BETTER WHEN ACCOMPANIED BY A SIDE ORDER OF CHEESE.

CHEESE. IS. EVERYTHING.

This book contains more than 40 recipes to help you celebrate this dreamy dairy. Every meal of the day — and all the snacks and sweets you can manage in between — can be given a welcome endorphin-enhancing cheese-boost. Cheese can be mixed into cakes and pies, loaded onto popcorn, spooned into bowls, and even stuffed inside donuts. Is there anything this wonderfood cannot do?

Why do we love cheese so much?

Studies have shown that eating cheese releases endorphins, which have a similar effect on the brain as opiates. Maybe that's why we have such crazy dreams when we eat too much cheese — or perhaps that's just a myth. Or maybe it's simply that cheese is the answer to all of life's deepest desires...

So ... what *is* cheese?

So to really understand what cheese can bring to the table, we first need to know what it actually is. Let's start with some science ...

Cheese is a milk product. So far, so good. During the process of making cheese, enzymes are added to the milk that cause it to coagulate. Then the solids (the curds) are pressed into cheese, and the liquids (the whey) are drained off.

Most cheeses are made from cow's milk — but goat, sheep and buffalo (that gorgeous puffy pillow of mozzarella!) are also common.

The nuances in processing, the type of milk used (and what the animal ate), and how the cheese is stored and aged all come into play, resulting in hundreds and hundreds of varieties of cheese, each one as glorious as the next.

MAIN TYPES OF CHEESE

Here's a quick guide to help you on your way to culinary cheese perfection.

Hard and semi-hard cheeses

With hard cheeses, generally more of the cheese solids are separated out, before they are loaded into tight moulds and aged for a long time, which is why they tend to be the most expensive. Parmesan, pecorino, gruyère, cheddar, monterey jack, red leicester, manchego and Swiss cheeses like emmental are the most common hard and semi-hard cheeses we all know and love. They usually have a fairly strong flavour, and are generally good all-round melters. Any of these has a warm and welcome home in a toastie — preferably in combination with one another. It's a good idea to grate hard cheeses before cooking them, so they melt more evenly.

Semi-soft cheeses

These are — you guessed it! — a bit softer than hard cheeses. They contain more moisture and are generally a bit gentler on the palate. Our favourite stringy cheese, mozzarella, is a semi-soft cheese.

Soft cheeses

These include our squishy goat's cheeses, bries, camemberts, blue cheeses and crumbly fetas of the cheese board. They range in flavour from the stinkiest oozing camembert to the mildest, saltiest feta. They aren't the best melters since they tend to become very runny, but you can bake them whole quite successfully.

Ricotta and cream cheese are also soft cheeses.

Mould, glorious mould ...

While all cheese is essentially soured milk, during the ripening, maturing stage — which can take anything from just a few days, to many years underground in the dark, in the case of parmesan — many cheeses develop a rind. This furry outer layer is found on our most beloved soft cheeses, camembert and brie.

Some cheeses are also actively encouraged to grow mould inside them, which gives the final cheese a strong, punchy flavour. Mould-ripened cheeses, also known as 'blue' cheeses, include stilton and gorgonzola. You don't need much of these blue, mouldy cheeses to feel their impact; they stand up well to stronger flavours such as meats, and are the heroes in salads and even burgers. They also seem to go well with walnuts for some reason!

CHEESE
SNACKS

WASABI & PARMESAN POPCORN

MOVIE NIGHT ALWAYS NEEDS MORE CHEESE! AND POPCORN! NEXT TIME YOU SETTLE DOWN WITH A CHEESY, CORNY ROM-COM FULL OF HOTTIES, THIS CHEESY HOT POPCORN HAS YOU COVERED.

SERVES 4 (OR 2 VERY GENEROUSLY)

3 tablespoons oil (coconut, vegetable, sunflower, rapeseed are best)
100 g (3½ oz/¾ cup) popcorn kernels
3 tablespoons butter
25 g (1 oz/¼ cup) grated parmesan
1 tablespoon wasabi powder

Heat the oil in a large lidded saucepan over medium heat. To test if it's hot enough, throw in a couple of corn kernels and put the lid back on. If they pop, you're ready to go!

Remove the pan from the heat. Tip in the rest of the kernels, shaking the pan to spread them out in an even layer, then put the lid back on. Wait for 30 seconds, then place back over the heat and let them start popping, shaking the pan regularly to keep them moving around.

While the corn is popping, melt the butter in a small saucepan — let it turn just a little bit brown, but do not burn it. Mix the parmesan with the wasabi powder.

When the popping has slowed down, with a few seconds between each pop, tip the popcorn into a large bowl (or separate bowls). Pour the melted butter over and use your hands or large spoons to toss and coat it in the buttery goodness.

Sprinkle with the cheese and wasabi mix and toss to coat again. The heat of the corn will melt the cheese, making every mouthful a umami delight as the molten cheese gets lost in the pockets of corn.

BACON-WRAPPED MINI MOZZARELLA BALLS

CHEESE AND BACON: DOES A BETTER PAIRING EXIST? THE DIPPING SAUCE IS SPICY YET COOLING — ANOTHER TANTALISING COMBO. YOU CAN USE REDUCED-FAT SOUR CREAM AND/OR MAYONNAISE IN THE DIPPING SAUCE IF YOU PREFER, BUT WHEN YOU'RE DEALING WITH CHEESE AND BACON, IT'S BEST TO GO ALL IN.

MAKES 12

12 mini mozzarella balls
12 rashers (slices) of unsmoked
    streaky bacon
1 tablespoon olive oil

Spicy dipping sauce
150 g (5½ oz) sour cream
1 tablespoon mayonnaise
1 teaspoon sriracha hot sauce
generous squeeze of lemon juice

Wrap each of the mozzarella balls carefully in a bacon slice, making sure the cheese is completely covered so it doesn't ooze out during cooking. Secure each one in place with a cocktail stick.

Heat the olive oil in a frying pan over medium heat and fry the balls for 8–10 minutes, turning them over every so often using tongs so they brown on all sides. You want the bacon to be nice and crispy.

While the bacon-mozzarella balls are cooking, mix the spicy dipping sauce ingredients together in a small serving dish.

Serve the bacon-clad mozzarella balls hot from the pan, with the sauce for dipping into. Watch out for the molten cheese!

CHEESY EGG HOLE BREAD

THE LESS SAID IN PUBLIC ABOUT THIS BUTTERY, CHEESY, HOT-FROM-THE-PAN, BREADY EGG ADVENTURE, THE BETTER. THIS IS A SECRET NIGHT-TIME MEAL THAT YOU SHOULDN'T TELL ANYONE ABOUT — WHICH IS WHY IT ONLY MAKES ENOUGH FOR ONE. THIS IS JUST BETWEEN YOU AND YOUR PAN.

SERVES 1

1–2 tablespoons butter
1 slice of bread, with a hole cut in
    the middle
1 free-range egg
splash of worcestershire sauce
small handful of grated cheese, such
    as cheddar, gruyère, red leicester

Melt the butter in a non-stick frying pan over medium heat. Fry the slice of bread and the cut-out piece of bread on one side for a few minutes until crispy and nicely browned, then flip them both over. If the pan looks a bit dry, add some more butter. Remove the cut-out piece once browned, set aside and keep warm.

Crack the egg into the hole. Season the bread around the edge with a little worcestershire sauce and top with the cheese. Let the egg cook for a few minutes, until the white sets.

Use a spatula to lift the bread out of the pan, then carefully flip the bread over to cook briefly on the other side, to crisp up the cheese, and to cook the egg according to your yolky preference.

Devour straight away.

MOLTEN CHEESY CHIVE DOUGH BALLS

TRY TO SHARE THESE WARM, CHEESY POCKETS OF 'I-WANT-TO-EAT-THEM-ALL!' GOODNESS, AS THEY'RE MEANT FOR YOUR GUESTS TOO.

MAKES 25

80 g (2¾ oz) butter, plus extra
   for greasing
1 garlic clove, crushed
25 mini mozzarella balls
70 g (2½ oz) grated extra-mature
   cheddar
2 tablespoons chopped chives

For the dough
60 g (2 oz) butter
2 teaspoons fast-acting dried yeast
200 ml (7 fl oz) warm water
2 tablespoons caster (superfine)
   sugar
450 g (1 lb/3 cups) plain
   (all-purpose) flour, plus extra
   for dusting
pinch of sea salt
3 tablespoons olive oil

Start by making the dough. Melt the butter in a small saucepan, remove from the heat and leave to cool. Meanwhile, in a cup or small bowl, mix the yeast with the warm water and a pinch of the sugar. Give it a swirl and leave it somewhere warm for 10 minutes. The yeast should start to foam — that's how you'll know it's *alive*!

In a large bowl, combine the flour, remaining sugar and salt. Slowly add the melted butter and the olive oil, mixing with your hands, then add the yeasty water. Keep working it in with your hands to bring it all together into a soft dough. The dough should feel quite soft, but not too dry and not too sticky; sprinkle in a little more flour if it's very sticky, and a splash more water if it's a little dry. When it has formed a dough, cover with plastic wrap and leave for 10 minutes.

Turn the dough out onto a lightly floured work surface and start to knead it. Keep kneading for 10 minutes, by which point the dough will have a firmer consistency. If the dough sticks to your work surface, sprinkle over some more flour, but don't add too much or your dough will become dry. Put the dough back in the bowl and cover with plastic wrap. Leave in a warm place for 1–1¼ hours. It should have roughly doubled in size by this stage.

Preheat the oven to 200°C/400°F (fan-forced) and grease two baking trays with a little extra butter. Melt the remaining butter and let cool, then mix in the garlic.

Knead the risen dough very briefly — just 30 seconds or so — then divide it into 25 even portions. Flatten them slightly, place a mozzarella ball on each one, wrap it up in the dough and pinch the edges tightly to seal. Roll the balls gently to smooth the surface, then place on the baking trays, pinched side down.

Brush with some of the garlicky melted butter, then sprinkle with the grated cheddar and half the chives. Bake for 10–15 minutes, until golden brown and bubbling. Remove from the oven and immediately brush with the remaining garlic butter. Sprinkle with the rest of the chives and serve hot.

MINI MACARONI CROQUETTES WITH BLOODY MARY DIPPING SAUCE

IT'S HARD TO IMPROVE ON A STEAMING HOT BOWL OF EXTRA-CHEESY MACARONI, BUT THESE CRISPY, CRUNCHY MOLTEN LITTLE BITES MAKE AN EXCELLENT ATTEMPT. RATHER THAN SHAPING THE MIXTURE INTO CROQUETTES, YOU CAN ALSO TIP THE MAC AND CHEESE MIXTURE INTO A BAKING DISH AND COOK IT IN A 200°C/400°F (FAN-FORCED) OVEN FOR ABOUT 15–20 MINUTES; IT WILL SERVE FOUR, GENEROUSLY, AS A SIDE DISH.

MAKES ABOUT 30 CROQUETTES

300 g (10½ oz) macaroni
1¼ tablespoons butter
2 tablespoons plain (all-purpose) flour
300 ml (10 fl oz) milk
125 g (4½ oz/1 cup) grated mature cheddar
1 teaspoon chilli flakes
3 tablespoons chopped jalapeño chillies
vegetable oil, for deep-frying

For crumbing
75 g (2¾ oz/½ cup) plain (all-purpose) flour
1 teaspoon chilli flakes
sea salt and freshly ground black pepper
1 free-range egg
75 g (2¾ oz) breadcrumbs, made from day-old bread
3 tablespoons grated parmesan

In a large saucepan of salted boiling water, cook the macaroni for 8–10 minutes, or until it is nearly cooked, but still retains a little firmness. Drain well, then return to the cooking pan.

While the pasta is bubbling, melt the butter in a saucepan. Stir in the flour and cook for about 30 seconds, then slowly add the milk. Keep stirring to make a smooth, thick roux, then stir in the cheddar to make a rich, cheesy sauce. Stir in the chilli flakes and jalapeños and remove from the heat.

When the macaroni is ready, stir the cheesy sauce through. Allow to cool to room temperature, then chill in the fridge for about 1 hour.

When the macaroni cheese has firmed up, line a baking tray with baking paper, and line up three shallow bowls in front of you, ready for crumbing. Tip the flour into one, and season with the chilli flakes and salt and pepper. Into the second, crack the egg and beat it lightly. In the third, combine the breadcrumbs and parmesan and season with pepper.

One at a time, using your hands, shape the macaroni cheese into small logs. Roll them first in the seasoned flour, then dip in the egg briefly, then coat in the breadcrumbs, making sure they're well covered in crumbs. Lay them on the lined baking tray then chill in the fridge for 20 minutes to help set the coating.

While they are chilling, make the dipping sauce. Heat the passata in a small saucepan over medium heat for about 5–10 minutes, until thickened to a dipping consistency. Stir in the remaining ingredients and season to taste with salt and pepper. Heat for a few more minutes, then taste and add more worcestershire sauce, hot chilli sauce or lemon juice — it should be a bit hotter than you'd normally like, because you'll be dipping all that cheesy goodness in it. Leave to cool to room temperature.

Bloody Mary dipping sauce
250 ml (8½ fl oz/1 cup) tomato passata (puréed tomatoes)
1 tablespoon worcestershire sauce
a few drops of hot chilli sauce or Tabasco
juice of ½ lemon
2 tablespoons vodka (optional)
sea salt and freshly ground black pepper

When the croquettes have chilled, heat about 10 cm (4 inches) of oil in a deep saucepan over medium-high heat to 185°C (365°F), or until a small piece of bread dropped in the oil fizzes and turns brown within 30 seconds. Keep an eye on the oil temperature so it doesn't get too high or drop too low; check the temperature using a kitchen thermometer, if you have one, as the croquettes won't crisp up properly if the oil's not hot enough.

Carefully lower the croquettes into the oil, no more than three or four at a time (depending on the size of your pan). Cook for about 2-3 minutes, turning them gently until they are brown and crispy all over. Use a thermometer to keep an eye on the temperature of the oil.

Carefully lift the croquettes out with a slotted spoon. Drain briefly on paper towel, then serve hot, with the dipping sauce.

CROQUE MONSIEUR (OR MADAME!) WITH CHILLI JAM

WHO SAYS GENDER IS FIXED? EVEN A CLASSICALLY ELEGANT MONSIEUR SOMETIMES FEELS LIKE BEING THE MADAME OF THE BALL. THE SIMPLEST INGREDIENTS PLAY A STARRING ROLE HERE, SO FOR A KNOCKOUT PERFORMANCE, MAKE SURE THEY'RE ALL GOOD QUALITY — ESPECIALLY THE BREAD.

MAKES 2

3-4 tablespoons butter
1 tablespoon plain (all-purpose) flour
4 thick slices of good white bread
100 ml (3½ fl oz) milk
150 g (5½ oz) grated gruyère or cheddar
pinch of chilli flakes
2 tablespoons chilli jam or bacon jam
2-4 slices of prosciutto (or try salami!), torn into strips

For the madame
1 tablespoon butter
4 quail eggs, or 2 free-range chicken eggs

Melt 1 tablespoon of the butter in a small saucepan and stir in the flour. Cook for 30 seconds, then add the milk slowly in a few batches, making sure the mixture is smooth and the milk is fully incorporated before adding the next lot. Cook for 4-5 minutes, until the sauce is of a good thick consistency, then stir in half the cheese and season with the chilli flakes.

Preheat the grill (broiler) to high. While you're keeping one eye on stirring and thickening the sauce, melt another 2 tablespoons of butter in a frying pan over medium–high heat. Add the bread — probably two slices at a time, depending on how big your pan is — and cook on one side only for 2-3 minutes, until it starts to brown and crisp up. You may need to add more butter to the pan; cook the remaining slices in the same way.

Transfer two slices of the bread, cooked side down, to a baking tray, and spread with the jam. Top with the prosciutto and the rest of the grated cheese. Grill for a minute or two, just to melt the cheese, then top with the other slices of bread, placing them cooked side up, and pressing down lightly. Pour the cheesy sauce over and return to the grill for 3-4 minutes, until golden and outrageously gooey.

While the monsieurs are finishing up, you can get your madame ready, if you're feeling so inclined. Melt the butter in a frying pan over medium heat and fry the eggs to your liking — ideally, runny yolks all round. When the sandwiches are ready, top with the eggs and serve.

DEEP-FRIED BEETROOT
& GOAT'S CHEESE BALLS

YOU *CAN* USE PRE-PACKAGED GRATED BEETROOT HERE, BUT IT USUALLY COMES WITH VINEGAR AND SPICES, WHICH WILL MAKE THESE LOVELY MORSELS TASTE DIFFERENT. IT REALLY DOESN'T TAKE LONG TO PEEL AND GRATE A RAW ONE — JUST WEAR GLOVES SO YOU DON'T LOOK LIKE A MURDERER ...

MAKES 8

185 g (6½ oz) freshly grated
  beetroot (beet)
sea salt and freshly ground black
  pepper
70 g (2½ oz) soft goat's cheese
50 g (1¾ oz/⅓ cup) plain
  (all-purpose) flour
1 free-range egg
40 g (1½ oz) breadcrumbs, made
  from day-old bread
2 tablespoons grated parmesan
vegetable oil, for deep-frying

Put the grated beetroot in a bowl. Squeeze out as much juice as you can; you may want to wear gloves for this! Season with salt and pepper, then mix in the goat's cheese. Scoop out eight little balls of the mixture and roll each one into a ball, about 2 cm (¾ inch) in diameter — don't make them any larger than this, or they won't cook through. Put them in the fridge while you get the next bit ready.

Line up three bowls in front of you. Into one, tip the flour and season with salt and pepper. Into the second, crack the egg and beat it lightly. In the third, combine the breadcrumbs and parmesan and season with pepper.

Roll the cheese and beetroot balls first in the flour, then dip in the egg briefly, then coat in the breadcrumbs, making sure they're well covered in crumbs. Transfer to a plate and chill in the fridge for 30 minutes.

In a deep saucepan, measuring about 20 cm (8 inches) across, heat 7–8 cm (2¾–3¼ inches) of oil over medium–high heat. Keep an eye on the oil temperature so it doesn't get too high or drop too low; you need it to stay around 185°C (365°F), or until a small piece of bread dropped in the oil fizzes and turns brown within 30 seconds. (Check the temperature using a kitchen thermometer, if you have one, as the balls won't crisp up properly if the oil's not hot enough.)

Carefully lower the balls into the oil, no more than three at a time, or the oil will cool down and they'll be soggy. Cook for about 2 minutes, turning them gently until they are brown and crispy all over, then carefully lift them out with a slotted spoon and drain on paper towel. Serve hot.

WARM CHEESE & CARAMELISED ONION DIP

THIS CREAMY, SWEET AND TANGY DIP IS PERFECT WITH BREADSTICKS, CRACKERS, HUNKS OF LIGHTLY TOASTED BREAD, AND CRUNCHY VEGETABLES SUCH AS BROCCOLI STALKS AND CELERY STICKS — OR TRY DOLLOPING IT OVER NACHOS.

SERVES 4

2 tablespoons butter
1 large red onion, finely chopped
1 teaspoon thyme leaves
freshly ground black pepper
1 tablespoon balsamic vinegar
145 g (5 oz) grated gruyère
90 g (3 oz) mascarpone
80 g (2¾ oz) sour cream

Melt the butter in a frying pan over medium–low heat. Cook the onion with the thyme and a good grind of black pepper for 20–30 minutes, stirring often, until the onion is soft, sweet and slightly sticky.

Turn the heat up to medium, then stir in the vinegar. Allow to bubble and become even stickier for a couple of minutes, stirring often so the mixture doesn't burn, and scraping up any delicious sticky bits from the bottom of the pan. Remove from the heat and allow to cool.

Meanwhile, preheat the oven to 200°C/400°F (fan-forced).

Place most of the gruyère in a bowl, reserving about 25 g (1 oz) for sprinkling over the dip. Add the mascarpone and sour cream and mix together. Season with black pepper, then stir the caramelised onion through.

Spoon the cheesy onion mixture into a 500 ml (17 fl oz/2 cup) capacity ovenproof dish (or four small ramekins) and sprinkle with the reserved gruyère. Bake for 10–15 minutes, until bubbling and lightly golden on top.

Serve hot, with your choice of dipping ingredients.

HALOUMI CHIPS

FRIED CHEESE: SURELY WHAT THE GODS SNACK ON EVERY DAY? LEMON THYME SETTLES IN WELL WITH THE GREEK FEEL, BUT YOU CAN JUST USE REGULAR THYME.

SERVES 2–3 AS A SIDE OR SNACK

160 g (5½ oz) block of haloumi
50 g (1¾ oz/⅓ cup) plain
    (all-purpose) flour
1 teaspoon lemon thyme leaves
freshly ground black pepper
1 tablespoon olive oil

Heavenly dipping sauce
75 g (2¾ oz) sour cream
1 teaspoon hot sauce

Cut the haloumi into chips about 1 cm (½ inch) thick. Don't make them too thick as they won't warm through properly as they cook, but don't make them too thin or they'll melt away into a gooey mess.

Season the flour with the thyme leaves and black pepper, then use it to coat the haloumi logs all over.

Heat the olive oil in a frying pan over medium heat and fry the haloumi chips for 4–5 minutes, turning them often, until browned and crispy all over. You may need to do this in a few batches, depending on the size of your pan.

Mix together the dipping sauce ingredients and serve with the haloumi chips, hot from the pan.

TARTINES

A DEPARTURE HERE INTO A MORE SOPHISTICATED SETTING ... REMEMBER THAT YOU'RE TEMPORARILY FRENCH (READ: CLASSY), SO USE A SMALL LOAF FOR THESE ELEGANT NIBBLES. THEY ARE LITTLE MORSELS, NOT GIANT OPEN TOASTIES. INSTEAD OF TOASTING THE BREAD, YOU COULD FRY IT IN A PAN WITH A LITTLE OLIVE OIL UNTIL CRISPY.

SPINACH, COMTÉ & CAMEMBERT WITH STICKY RED ONION TARTINE

MAKES 4

1 tablespoon olive oil
1 red onion, finely chopped
1 tablespoon balsamic vinegar
100 g (3½ oz/2 cups) baby English
   spinach leaves
1 tablespoon butter
squeeze of lemon juice
4 thick slices of sourdough
75 g (2¾ oz) grated comté
50 g (1¾ oz) camembert, sliced
4 walnuts, lightly crushed
a few thyme leaves

Heat the olive oil in a frying pan and cook the onion over medium–low heat for 15–20 minutes, stirring regularly, until sticky and sweet. Stir in the vinegar and leave to bubble for a few minutes, to become even more sticky and delicious, stirring so the mixture doesn't burn. Remove from the heat and set aside.

Wilt the spinach in a large frying pan and cook over medium heat for about 2 minutes, until all the liquid has evaporated. Tip into a sieve and press with the back of a spoon to remove even more liquid. Return to the pan with the butter and a splash of lemon juice and cook for a few minutes.

Meanwhile, preheat the grill (broiler) to medium. Toast the bread on one side.

Spread the onion mixture over the untoasted side of the bread. Top with the spinach, then the grated comté, then the camembert slices. Return to the grill to melt the cheese.

Serve scattered with the walnuts and thyme leaves.

GOAT'S CHEESE & ROASTED CAPSICUM TARTINE

MAKES 4

4 thick slices of a farmhouse loaf
1 garlic clove, peeled and pricked
   with a fork
125 g (4½ oz) roasted capsicums
   (bell peppers), in oil
8 kalamata olives, halved
sea salt and freshly ground black
   pepper
120 g (4½ oz) log of goat's cheese,
   cut lengthways into 4 thick slices
pinch of chilli flakes

Preheat the grill (broiler) to medium. Toast the bread slices under the grill on one side only.

Remove the bread from the grill and rub the untoasted side with the garlic clove. Drain the roasted capsicums, reserving the oil, and arrange them over the bread.

Top with the olives, a sprinkling of salt and pepper, and the cheese slices. Sprinkle with the chilli flakes, then heat under the grill to melt the cheese. Serve hot, drizzled with a little of the reserved oil from the capsicums.

REBLOCHON MOUNTAIN TARTINE

MAKES 4

100 g (3½ oz) bacon lardons
(or chopped pancetta or chunky
bacon)
1½ teaspoons olive oil
a few thyme sprigs
4 thick slices of a farmhouse
white loaf
1 tablespoon dijon mustard
1 onion, thinly sliced
120 g (4½ oz) reblochon, sliced
2 teaspoons chopped cornichons
or gherkins (pickles)

Fry the bacon lardons and thyme sprigs in the olive oil over medium heat for about 10 minutes, or until browned, crispy and a little bit sticky.

Meanwhile, preheat the grill (broiler) to medium. Toast the bread on one side under the grill. Turn the bread over and spread with the mustard. Top with the onion slices, then the cheese. Toast for a few more minutes, to melt the cheese.

Plate the tartines and serve warm, scattered with the lardons and cornichons.

LEMON RICOTTA, ROASTED TOMATO & GREEN HERB PESTO TARTINE

MAKES 4

10 juicy vine-ripened tomatoes,
quartered
2 tablespoons olive oil
sea salt and freshly ground black
pepper
125 g (4½ oz/½ cup) ricotta
zest of 1 lemon
4 thick slices of sourdough bread
freshly ground black pepper

Green herb pesto
35 g (1¼ oz) almonds
25 g (1 oz/½ cup firmly packed)
basil leaves
20 g (¾ oz/1 cup firmly packed)
mint leaves
2 tablespoons thyme leaves
35 g (1¼ oz/⅓ cup) grated parmesan
1 garlic clove, crushed
80–90 ml (2½–3 fl oz) olive oil
sea salt and freshly ground black
pepper
squeeze of lemon juice

Preheat the oven to 200°C/400°F (fan-forced). Arrange the tomato quarters on a baking tray, toss in 1 tablespoon of the olive oil and season with salt and pepper. Roast for 15–20 minutes, until softened and a little brown and sticky around the edges.

Meanwhile, make a start on the pesto. Toast the almonds in a dry frying pan over medium heat for 30 seconds, shaking the pan regularly; watch them carefully to make sure they don't get too dark. Tip onto a plate to cool slightly.

In a mini blender, blitz the toasted almonds with the herbs, parmesan and garlic to roughly break them up. With the blender running, pour in the olive oil until you have a loose consistency; you may not need all the oil. Season to taste with salt and pepper and a squeeze of lemon juice. Set aside.

Mix the ricotta with the lemon zest and set aside.

When the tomatoes are done, remove them from the oven and leave to cool a little while you toast the sourdough. Drizzle the remaining olive oil over the sourdough and sprinkle with black pepper.

Spread the sourdough toasts with a thick layer of the lemon ricotta. Top with the tomatoes, drizzle with the pesto and serve.

GIANT CHEESE BALL

PUT THIS IN THE MIDDLE OF THE TABLE AND DIG IN WITH CRACKERS, CELERY STICKS, CORN CHIPS, YOUR HANDS ... YOU CAN ALSO MOULD THE CHEESE INTO WONDERFUL SHAPES LIKE A PUMPKIN OR A CAT OR A HEAD, AND DECORATE ACCORDINGLY.

SERVES 8–10

250 g (9 oz) creamy cheese, such as mascarpone, cream cheese, garlic cream cheese

150 g (5½ oz) grated mature cheddar

50 g (1¾ oz/⅓ cup) grated mozzarella (or you can just use 200 g/7 oz grated cheddar)

50 g (1¾ oz) blue cheese

3 tablespoons chopped chives

3 tablespoons chopped flat-leaf (Italian) parsley

60 g (2 oz) chopped nuts (almonds, walnuts, pecans or a mixture are all good)

freshly ground black pepper

pinch of chilli flakes (optional)

2 tablespoons maple syrup

1 teaspoon dijon mustard

6 rashers (slices) of back bacon

Mix the four cheeses together in a bowl until evenly combined. Mix in the chives, half the parsley, and 2 tablespoons of the chopped nuts; season with pepper and the chilli flakes, if using. Shape into a neat ball, then wrap in plastic wrap and chill in the fridge for 2½ hours to firm up.

Meanwhile, preheat the grill (broiler) to high. Mix together the maple syrup and mustard to make a glaze for the bacon. Lay the bacon on a grill rack, with a foil-lined tray underneath to catch the drips. Brush the glaze over the top of the bacon, then grill for about 5 minutes, or until crispy, turning the bacon over halfway through to brush some glaze on the other side. Cool, then chill in the fridge.

When the cheese ball is firm, crumble the bacon into small pieces and mix together with the remaining nuts and parsley. Spread out in a shallow bowl or on a plate.

Roll the cheese ball through the nutty bacon mixture to coat it all over, then wrap again in plastic wrap until ready to serve. The cheese ball is best enjoyed the day it is made, or ideally within a few hours of coating.

HOISIN CHINESE-DUCK PIZZA PINWHEELS

LIKE A CHINESE TAKEAWAY IN A SQUISHY ROLL WITH EXTRA CHEESE. SAY, WHAT?! IT'S ALL YOUR FAVOURITE THINGS IN ONE PLACE. THE DOUGH IS A CINCH TO MAKE, BUT FOR EASE AND SPEED, YOU COULD USE READY-ROLLED PUFF PASTRY INSTEAD.

MAKES 12

For the dough
300 g (10¼ oz/2 cups) self-raising flour, plus extra for dusting
pinch of sea salt
pinch of chilli flakes
90 g (3 oz) butter, cut into cubes
500 ml (17 fl oz/2 cups) milk

For the filling
80 ml (2½ fl oz/⅓ cup) hoisin sauce
125 g (4½ oz) cooked duck breast, diced
1 teaspoon Chinese five-spice
1 small red onion, finely chopped
small handful of chopped coriander (cilantro) leaves
175 g (6 oz) grated mozzarella
75 g (2¾ oz) grated cheddar
1 free-range egg, beaten

Preheat the oven to 200°C/400°F (fan-forced). Line a baking tray with baking paper.

To make the dough, sift the flour into a bowl and stir in the salt and chilli flakes. Rub in the butter until the mixture looks like fine breadcrumbs. Add the milk a little at a time, and bring the mixture together with your hands, into a soft dough. Don't let it become too wet — you may not need all of the milk, or you may need a splash more.

Knead the dough on a lightly floured work surface for a few minutes, then roll it out to form a rectangle about 1 cm (½ inch) thick.

Spread the dough with the hoisin sauce, then scatter over the duck, five-spice, onion, coriander and cheese, reserving a handful of the mozzarella and cheddar.

Carefully roll up the dough like a Swiss roll (jelly roll), then cut into 12 even slices, about 2 cm (¾ inch) thick. Lay them on the baking tray, cut side up, keeping them quite close together. Brush lightly with the beaten egg, then sprinkle with the rest of the cheese.

Bake for 15–20 minutes, until lightly golden and cooked through. Enjoy warm.

LUXURY CHEESE TOASTIE

THERE'S NOTHING WRONG WITH A BASIC CHEESE SANDWICH, BUT WHY NOT LIVE THE HIGH LIFE NOW AND THEN?
A COUPLE OF RULES FOR THE RITZY: DON'T SLICE THE BREAD TOO THICK OR HAVE THE PAN TOO HOT, OR YOUR BREAD
WILL TOAST BUT YOUR CHEESE WON'T MELT — AND WHAT'S A TOASTIE WITHOUT MELTED CHEESE?

SERVES 1

4 rashers (slices) of streaky bacon
2 tablespoons butter, plus extra
    for spreading
2 slices of fluffy white bread or
    sourdough (nothing too holey)
1 tablespoon wholegrain mustard
4 slices of gruyère or comté, no
    more than 5 mm (¼ inch) thick
3 tablespoons sauerkraut, drained
sea salt and freshly ground black
    pepper

Grill (broil) the bacon until crispy.

Butter one side of each piece of bread. Spread the mustard over the other side. Place two cheese slices on each mustard-covered side of bread, making sure you cover the whole piece of bread, so there are no gaps in the cheese (rather than going for a double layer of cheese).

Top one cheese-covered slice with the bacon, then spoon on the sauerkraut. Season with salt and pepper.

Close the sandwich with the other piece of bread, buttered-side up, sauerkraut meeting cheese.

Melt the butter in a frying pan over medium heat and cook the sandwich for about 4 minutes on each side, until the bread is browned and crispy, and the cheese has melted inside. Press it down with a spatula every so often to make it hold together, and gently move it about in the pan so it cooks evenly underneath.

Remove the toastie from the pan very carefully and give it a minute to chill out. Molten cheese can get as hot as the sun, and you don't want a cheese-burn incident! Now slice in half, devour and fall in love.

CHEESE
SIDES & SALADS

CHEESY ASPARAGUS & ZUCCHINI SPEARS

EVEN AN UNSUSPECTING, INNOCENT SIDE DISH OF HEALTHY VEG CAN BE COVERED IN CHEESE AND BAKED TO PERFECTION. CHEESE, YOU'VE DONE IT AGAIN.

SERVES 4 AS A SIDE DISH

2 zucchini (courgettes)
12 asparagus spears, ends trimmed
2 tablespoons olive oil
sea salt and freshly ground black pepper
pinch of chilli flakes (optional)
50 g (1¾ oz) bacon lardons (or diced pancetta or chunky bacon)
1 tablespoon butter
1½ teaspoons plain (all-purpose) flour
80 ml (2½ fl oz/⅓ cup) milk
2 tablespoons pouring (single/light) cream
50 g (1¾ oz/⅓ cup) grated extra-mature cheddar
100 g (3½ oz) grated gruyère
2 tablespoons grated parmesan

Preheat the oven to 200°C/400°F (fan-forced). Line a baking tray with baking paper or foil.

Cut each zucchini into quarters lengthways, then cut each quarter in half lengthways too, to give 16 zucchini spears. Trim them so they are the same length as the asparagus spears. Toss the zucchini in 1½ teaspoons of the olive oil. Season with salt and pepper, and the chilli flakes, if using. Spread the pieces out on the baking tray and bake for 10 minutes, then turn them over and bake for another 5 minutes.

Quickly toss the asparagus with another 1½ teaspoons of the olive oil. Now bake them with the zucchini for 5 minutes or so; the zucchini pieces should be softened, but still holding their shape. Remove from the oven and leave to cool to room temperature.

Heat the remaining oil in a small frying pan and cook the bacon lardons, stirring regularly, over medium heat for about 10 minutes, until crispy and brown. Tip onto paper towel to drain.

While the bacon is cooking, make the cheesy sauce. Melt the butter in a small saucepan and stir in the flour. Cook, stirring, for 30 seconds, then add the milk slowly in a few batches, making sure the mixture is smooth and the milk is fully incorporated before adding the next lot. Cook for about 5 minutes, until the sauce is a good thick consistency, then stir in the cream, all the cheddar, and half the gruyère. Season with pepper and fold the cooked bacon lardons through. Set aside but keep warm.

Preheat your grill (broiler) to high. Line another baking tray with baking paper. Arrange the zucchini and asparagus on the baking tray, alternating the veggies; it looks pretty if you have half the spears at one end and half at the other, with their cut ends in the middle.

Dust with the parmesan, all the way to the tips of the spears, then spoon the sauce over, leaving the tips showing. Top with the remaining gruyère and grill for a few minutes, until the cheesy sauce is golden and bubbling. Serve hot.

BURRATA, MINI MOZZARELLA BALLS & ROASTED TOMATO SALAD

A BURRATA IS BASICALLY A FANCY BALL OF MOZZARELLA FILLED WITH CREAM. I MEAN, SERIOUSLY. NO WONDER THOSE ITALIANS LIVE FOREVER. HERE IT IS GENTLY WARMED BY ITS FAVOURITE SUNSHINE PALS: SWEET AND JUICY TOMATOES. AHH, A TASTE OF THE MED. I BET THEY EAT LIKE THIS ALL THE TIME.

SERVES 4 AS A SIDE DISH

600 g (1 lb 5 oz) tomatoes (a mix of cherry and larger ones work well)
3 tablespoons olive oil
5 garlic cloves, roughly sliced
2-3 rosemary sprigs
bunch of thyme sprigs
sea salt and freshly ground black pepper
125 g (4½ oz) mini mozzarella balls
bunch of basil, leaves picked
1 burrata (or large mozzarella ball)

Preheat the oven to 180°C/350°F (fan-forced). If you are using larger tomatoes, slice them thickly. Arrange all the tomatoes in a baking dish, in a roughly single layer. Drizzle with the olive oil, give them a little toss, then hide the garlic, rosemary and thyme between the tomatoes. Season generously with salt and pepper.

Bake for 20-25 minutes, until the tomatoes have softened and are starting to brown and become a bit sticky round the edges.

Remove from the oven and mix through the mozzarella balls and basil — the heat will start to melt the cheese and wilt the leaves.

Spoon into a large serving dish, then top with the burrata. Serve drizzled with the tomato juices from the baking dish.

CELERIAC, SWEET POTATO & PANCETTA GRATIN

A RICH AND CREAMY, CRAZILY COMFORTING BAKE — COVERED WITH CRUNCHY BACON, INSTEAD OF BORING BREADCRUMBS. YET ANOTHER WAY TO GET THOSE BESTIES, CHEESE AND BACON, TO HANG OUT ON YOUR PLATE.

SERVES 4–6 AS A SIDE,
OR 4 AS A MAIN WITH SALAD

2 tablespoons butter, plus extra
    for greasing
400 g (14 oz) sweet potato, peeled
200 g (7 oz) celeriac, peeled
100 ml (3½ fl oz) thick (double/
    heavy) cream
2 tablespoons roughly chopped
    tarragon
1 tablespoon chopped thyme
sea salt and freshly ground black
    pepper
200 g (7 oz) grated extra-mature
    cheddar
100 g (3½ oz) red leicester, sliced
1 tablespoon olive oil
150 g (5½ oz) pancetta, diced
    (or use bacon lardons)
3 spring onions (scallions), chopped
large handful of breadcrumbs, made
    from day-old bread
25 g (1 oz/¼ cup) grated parmesan

Preheat the oven to 200°C/400°F (fan-forced). Butter a large oval baking dish, measuring about 22 cm x 30 cm (8¾ inches x 12 inches).

Melt the butter in a small saucepan then allow to cool while preparing the vegetables.

Slice the sweet potato into thin discs — about 2–3 mm (⅛ inch). Do the same with the celeriac, making sure the slices are roughly the same size. Mix together in a bowl with the melted butter, cream, tarragon and thyme. Season with salt and pepper.

Layer the vegetables in the baking dish, with the cheese between the layers, but reserving about half the cheddar. Cover with foil and bake for 35–40 minutes, then remove the foil and cook for another 5–10 minutes. The sweet potato and celeriac should be soft when poked with a knife, and the sauce should be rich and creamy.

While the gratin is in the oven, heat the olive oil in a frying pan over medium–high heat and fry the pancetta for about 5 minutes, until lightly browned — but don't let it become crispy. Toss it into a bowl and leave to cool a little, then mix in the spring onion, breadcrumbs, parmesan and reserved cheddar.

Remove the foil from the gratin and spoon the pancetta mixture over. Cook, uncovered, for a further 15 minutes or so, until the cheese melts on top, the breadcrumbs and spring onion brown lightly, and the pancetta crisps up. Leave to sit for about 5 minutes before ploughing in.

GRILLED CORN ON THE COB SMOTHERED IN A CREAMY BLUE CHEESE BUTTER

JUICY CORN COBS ARE SLATHERED WITH A SPICY LIME BUTTER DURING GRILLING, THEN TOPPED WITH A CREAMY BLUE CHEESE MIXTURE THAT MELTS DREAMILY INTO THE TINY GAPS BETWEEN THE HOT KERNELS. YOU CAN ALSO USE MINI COBS FOR A BIGGER CROWD, OR GRILL THE CORN COBS ON A BARBECUE.

SERVES 4 AS A SIDE

50 g (1¾ oz) butter
2 teaspoons hot sauce
½ lime
4 corn cobs, husks and silks
 removed
65 g (2¼ oz) blue cheese, such
 as stilton
2 tablespoons sour cream
1 teaspoon thyme leaves
1 teaspoon chilli flakes
freshly ground black pepper

Preheat the grill (broiler) to medium-high. Meanwhile, melt the butter with the hot sauce in a small saucepan, then remove from the heat and squeeze in the lime juice.

Line a baking tray with foil and place it under the grill rack to catch any butter drips. Brush the corn cobs with the melted butter mixture. Grill, turning regularly, and brushing with the rest of the butter mixture, for 15–20 minutes, until the kernels are soft and look a little charred all over.

Meanwhile, in a small bowl, mix together the blue cheese, sour cream, thyme, chilli flakes and a good grind of black pepper; the mixture should be quite thick.

Serve the hot corn cobs topped with some of the blue cheese mixture, with the rest on the table for top-ups.

INDIVIDUAL CHEESE & ONION HASH BROWNS

AH, THE THREE AMIGOS: POTATO, CHEESE AND ONION. THESE LITTLE POTS OF JOY ARE GREAT WITH STEAK, OUR OTHER MEAL-TIME HERO.

SERVES 6 AS A SIDE

3 tablespoons butter, plus extra for greasing
2 onions, thinly sliced
400 g (14 oz) peeled and grated potato
large pinch of cayenne pepper
sea salt and freshly ground black pepper
3 tablespoons sour cream
125 g (4½ oz/1 cup) grated monterey jack (or other good melting cheese, such as gouda)
175 g (6 oz) grated Swiss cheese (such as gruyère or emmental)

Grease six 200 ml (7 fl oz) capacity ramekins with butter and set on a baking tray.

Melt 1 tablespoon of the butter in a frying pan over medium heat and cook the onion for 5–10 minutes, or until soft and a little golden. Tip onto a plate lined with paper towel to drain a little.

Meanwhile, dry the grated potato quite thoroughly with paper towel. Toss in a bowl with the cayenne pepper and a good sprinkling of salt and pepper.

Preheat the oven to 180°C/350°F (fan-forced).

Place the frying pan back over medium heat. Melt the remaining butter and cook the grated potato for about 10 minutes, stirring often, so it cooks and browns a little all over, but doesn't stick. The potato strands should be fairly dry and a little crispy at the edges. Scrape into a bowl, leave to cool a little, then mix in the sautéed onion, sour cream, monterey jack and half the Swiss cheese.

Pack the mixture into the ramekins, top with the remaining cheese and sprinkle with more pepper. Bake for 40 minutes, or until golden brown and bubbling on top. Leave to sit for a minute or two before serving — the ramekins will be really hot!

PULL-APART CHEESY GARLIC LOAF

GARLIC BREAD WILL NEVER BE THE SAME AGAIN. THIS ONE IS SO IRRESISTIBLE IT MAY RESULT IN AN INJURY BECAUSE YOU'LL WANT TO EAT IT SO QUICKLY. REMEMBER, MOLTEN CHEESE IS AS HOT AS THE SUN.

SERVES 4–6

750 g (1 lb 11 oz) loaf of sourdough bread
140 g (5 oz) red leicester
140 g (5 oz) fontina or emmental
150 g (5½ oz) block of mozzarella
75 g (2¾ oz) butter
3 garlic cloves, very finely chopped
2 tablespoons finely chopped parsley
freshly ground black pepper
pinch of chilli flakes (optional)

Preheat the oven to 180°C/350°F (fan-forced).

Using a sharp knife, cut the loaf of bread in criss-cross fashion (like a hedgehog), making the incisions about 1.5 cm (½ inch) apart, almost down to the bottom, leaving about 2 cm (¾ inch) intact at the base.

Wrap the bread in foil and bake for about 5 minutes, just while you grate the red leicester, and slice the fontina and mozzarella.

Remove the bread from the oven and unwrap it. Set aside a generous handful of grated cheese, then randomly push all the rest of the cheese into the gaps in the bread, alternating them so you'll end up with a cheesy lucky dip, and leaving some bits of cheese poking out the top.

Melt the butter in a small saucepan, then remove from the heat and mix in the garlic and parsley. Season with black pepper and chilli flakes, if using. Brush some of the garlic butter over the top of the loaf, then drizzle the rest into the cheese-filled pockets. Scatter the reserved grated cheese over the loaf.

Place on a baking tray and bake for about 20 minutes, until the cheese is so melty and a bit crispy on top that you can't wait a moment longer.

Enjoy the stretchy cheese as you pull chunks of bread out. Maybe make a video of it and post it on Instagram #cheesepull #cheeselove #almostburntmyfingersIcantgetatitfastenough ...

SWEET POTATO CHIPS WITH A SMOKY, CHEESY SAUCE

CHEESE. HEAVEN. IN. A. BOWL. THIS DISH IS IN THE SIDES CHAPTER, BUT YOU COULD EAT IT ON ITS OWN AS A SLIGHTLY GUILTY DINNER. WE WON'T TELL.

SERVES 2

1 large sweet potato, washed but unpeeled
1 tablespoon olive oil
sea salt and freshly ground black pepper
2 teaspoons thyme leaves
1 tablespoon butter
1 tablespoon plain (all-purpose) flour
150 ml (5 fl oz) milk
100 g (3½ oz) sour cream
½ teaspoon smoked paprika
60 g (2 oz/½ cup) grated mature cheddar
jalapeño chillies, to serve

Preheat the oven to 180°C/350°F (fan-forced). Cut the sweet potato into wedges, spread them out on a baking tray and toss in the olive oil. Season with salt and pepper and sprinkle with the thyme leaves. Bake for 25–30 minutes, turning occasionally.

Meanwhile, melt the butter in a saucepan over medium heat. Stir in the flour until lump-free. Keep stirring for about 30 seconds, then start to gradually add the milk, stirring until you have a smooth sauce before adding the next lot of milk. If you get some lumps, use a whisk to smooth them out. When you've added all the milk, stir the sour cream through. Cook for 5–10 minutes, until nicely thickened, then season with the smoked paprika and some pepper. Stir in the grated cheddar to make a smooth sauce, then allow to cool slightly.

When the chips are ready, put them in a bowl, scatter over some jalapeño chillies and pour the cheesy sauce over.

THREE-CHEESE CREAMY MASHED POTATOES

MMM, CREAMY CHEESY HOT MASHED POTATOES. THIS MASH IS FINISHED OFF UNDER THE GRILL, ADDING AN EXTRA LAYER OF CRISPY CHEESE GOODNESS ON TOP. LIFE DOESN'T GET MUCH BETTER.

SERVES 4–6 AS A SIDE

1 kg (2 lb 3 oz) mashing potatoes, such as russet, maris piper or coliban

sea salt and freshly ground black pepper

butter, for greasing

handful of breadcrumbs, made from day-old bread

2 tablespoons grated parmesan

1 tablespoon thyme leaves

40 g (1½ oz/⅓ cup) grated cheddar (or red leicester)

4 tablespoons mascarpone

2 tablespoons wholegrain mustard

35 g (1¼ oz/¼ cup) grated mozzarella

Peel the potatoes, cut them in half and place in a large saucepan. Cover with cold water, season with a pinch of salt and bring to the boil. Cook for 15–20 minutes, or until tender when poked with the tip of a sharp knife.

Meanwhile, butter a baking dish, measuring about 18 cm x 23 cm (7 inches x 9 inches), and about 6 cm (2½ inches) deep. In a bowl, mix the breadcrumbs with the parmesan, thyme and half the cheddar.

Preheat the grill (broiler) to high.

When the potatoes are cooked, drain well and return to the hot pan. Let them steam for a few seconds — soggy potatoes are no one's friend.

Mash the potatoes using a fork or potato masher. Mash in the mascarpone until smooth. Season with pepper — no salt — then stir in the mustard, mozzarella and remaining cheddar. Make sure the mash is very smooth and the cheese is well mixed through.

Spoon the mash into the baking dish. Scatter the breadcrumb mixture over and grill (broil) for 5 minutes, or until the topping is golden brown.

CHEESE MAINS

CHEDDAR & BEER SOUP

VERSIONS OF THIS SOUP WERE EATEN DURING THE MIDDLE AGES *FOR BREAKFAST.* TOO MUCH? NEVER! IF IT'S GOOD ENOUGH FOR MEDIEVAL KNIGHTS, THEN IT'S GOOD ENOUGH FOR YOU. WHERE'S MY HORSE?

SERVES 6

3 tablespoons butter

1 tablespoon olive oil

2 onions, chopped

1 celery stalk, chopped

1 carrot, chopped

1 red or green chilli, chopped

sea salt and freshly ground black pepper

6 large, crusty bread rolls (make sure they have firm crusts!)

3 tablespoons plain (all-purpose) flour

600 ml (20½ fl oz) vegetable or chicken stock

330 ml (11 fl oz) bottle of ale (a paler one, rather than a really dark ale)

100 ml (3½ fl oz) pouring (single/light) cream

300 g (10½ oz) grated extra-mature cheddar

1 teaspoon wholegrain mustard

juice of ½ lemon

thyme leaves, to garnish

Melt the butter with the olive oil in a large saucepan over medium heat. Cook the onion, celery, carrot and chilli for 25 minutes, stirring often, until the vegetables are soft. Season with salt and pepper.

Meanwhile, carefully slice the top off each bread roll. Scoop out the insides, leaving a good 2 cm (¾ inch) thick crust all the way round, so the soup won't leak out. If you're worried your buns may be too soft, give them a quick blast in a preheated 180°C/350°F (fan-forced) oven to harden them a little.

When the vegetables have softened, scatter the flour over and stir to coat, trying to get rid of any lumps of flour. Keep cooking and stirring for about 30 seconds. Slowly add the stock, a ladleful at a time, stirring to incorporate all the liquid before adding the next lot.

Bring to a simmer and cook for 15–20 minutes, until the vegetables are completely soft and the mixture has thickened to the consistency of thick cream.

Leave to cool slightly, then blitz the soup until smooth using a hand-held blender, or in batches in a regular blender, returning the soup to the pan.

Pour in the ale, then the cream, stirring well. Let the soup bubble over medium–low heat for about 15 minutes, or until it is heated through and reaches your desired consistency, then stir in the cheddar. Let it melt completely, then stir in the mustard and lemon juice. Taste and add more salt and pepper, lemon juice or mustard if needed.

Ladle the soup into your bread roll bowls, garnish with the thyme and serve immediately to your brave and gallant dining companions, at a preferably round table …

BUTTERNUT PUMPKIN & BLACK BEAN NACHOS

THIS HEALTHY-ISH CHEESE FEAST DOES SERVE FOUR, AND PROBABLY ALWAYS SHOULD, BUT IT ALSO SERVES TWO VERY HANDSOMELY ...

SERVES 4

800 g (1 lb 12 oz) butternut pumpkin (squash), peeled and cut into 1.5 cm (½ inch) chunks

2 tablespoons olive oil

sea salt and freshly ground black pepper

1 teaspoon cumin seeds

1 teaspoon dried oregano

1½ teaspoons ground coriander

1 teaspoon chilli flakes

100 g (3½ oz) monterey jack (or use gouda, muenster or a harder block of mozzarella)

100 g (3½ oz) strong cheddar

½ red onion

140 g (5 oz) tinned sweet corn kernels

230 g (8 oz) tinned black beans

200 g (7 oz) corn chips

small bunch (45 g/1½ oz) coriander (cilantro)

12–15 slices of jalapeño chilli (from a jar), drained

1 tomato

1 avocado

sour cream, to serve

lime wedges, to serve

Preheat the oven to 180°C/350°F (fan-forced).

Tip the pumpkin into a large roasting dish, about 30 cm (12 inches) square and 8 cm (3¼ inches) deep. Toss with the olive oil to coat, then season with salt and pepper. Scatter over the cumin seeds, oregano, ground coriander and chilli flakes. Use a large spoon to mix together well so the pumpkin is coated in the spicy oil.

Transfer to the oven and bake for 30–40 minutes, until the pumpkin is soft and sticky, stirring every 10 minutes to recoat the chunks in the spicy oil, and to ensure they cook evenly.

Meanwhile, grate the two cheeses and mix them together in a bowl. Finely chop the onion and place in another bowl. Rinse and drain the corn and black beans, then mix them together with the onion.

When the pumpkin is ready, tip it into a bowl, keeping the oven on. Layer half the corn chips in the same roasting dish you baked the pumpkin in. Top with half the corn and bean mixture, then half the roasted pumpkin. Use kitchen scissors to snip half the bunch of coriander over. Scatter with a few jalapeño slices and top with half the cheese mixture. Repeat the layers, except the remaining corn chips.

Return to the oven and bake for about 15 minutes, along with the remaining corn chips laid out on a separate baking tray, until the cheese is melted and everything is warmed through.

Meanwhile, dice the tomato finely and place in a bowl. Mash the avocado and mix it with the tomato.

Serve the nachos in a bowl, surrounded by corn chips, topped with the avocado mash, a generous dollop of sour cream and lime wedges for squeezing over.

SEVEN-CHEESE PIZZA

QUATTRO FORMAGGI IS FOR WIMPS. ENTER THE *SETTE FORMAGGI*, FOR HEROES! USING STICKS OF 'STRING' CHEESE IN THE PIZZA BASE MAY SEEM A CRIME, BUT THEIR RUBBERY TEXTURE MEANS THEY DON'T OOZE OUT AND MAKE A SOGGY MESS. IF YOU REALLY CAN'T FACE THEM, USE GRATED MOZZARELLA INSTEAD.

MAKES A 30 CM (12 INCH) PIZZA

125 g (4½ oz/½ cup) tomato pasta
    sauce
small pinch of chilli flakes
1 tablespoon oregano leaves
50 g (1¾ oz/⅓ cup) grated
    mozzarella
50 g (1¾ oz) grated cheddar
40 g (1½ oz) crumbled blue cheese
40 g (1½ oz) grated provolone
40 g (1½ oz) smoked gouda, diced
2 tablespoons grated parmesan

Start by making the pizza dough. In a cup or bowl, combine the yeast, sugar and warm water. Give it a swirl and leave it alone for 10 minutes somewhere warm. The yeast should start to foam — that's how you'll know it's alive.

Combine the flour, salt and cayenne pepper in a bowl. Drizzle the olive oil over. When the yeast is foamy, slowly add it to the flour, working it in with your hands to form a soft dough. If it's a little dry, add a splash more water; if it's a bit sticky, add a little more flour. Cover with plastic wrap and leave on the bench for 10 minutes.

Tip the dough onto a lightly floured work surface and knead for about 10 minutes, until smooth and stretchy. Return to the bowl, cover with plastic wrap and leave in a warm place for 1 hour, or until almost doubled in size.

Preheat the oven to 200°C/400°F (fan-forced) and get a large baking tray in there to heat up.

While the dough is rising, get your other ingredients ready. Take the string cheese and tease out the strings. Twist them together again to create longer, thinner, twisted cheese strings; these will go around the inside of your crust. Don't make them too big, or your crust will be huge and too cheesy to manage (there *is* such a thing!).

Mix the pasta sauce with the chilli flakes and half the oregano. Mix together the mozzarella and cheddar.

Cheesy crust pizza dough

2 teaspoons fast-acting dried yeast
2 teaspoons caster (superfine) sugar
150 ml (5 fl oz) warm water
320 g (11½ oz) plain (all-purpose)
    flour, plus extra for dusting
pinch of sea salt
1 teaspoon cayenne pepper
1 tablespoon olive oil
4–5 sticks of string cheese

When the dough has risen, knead it on a lightly floured work surface for 5 minutes. Roll the dough into a 35 cm (14 inch) circle. (If you're feeling fancy you can harness your inner Italian and spin it in the air … or maybe not!)

Transfer the pizza base to a pizza tray or large baking tray. Lay the twisted cheese strings all around the edge of the dough. Fold the pizza edge over the cheese, pinching it well to seal the cheese. Prick the dough with a fork.

Place the pizza tray on top of the hot baking tray. Transfer to the oven and bake for about 5 minutes — just until the pizza base is dry to the touch, but not starting to colour.

Remove from the oven to cool for a few minutes, then spread the tomato sauce around the middle. Sprinkle the crumbled blue cheese over, then the mozzarella and cheddar mixture. Top with the provolone and gouda, a sprinkling of parmesan, and the remaining oregano.

Bake for a further 15 minutes, or until the crust is golden and the cheese has melted. Cut into wedges to serve.

CHIPOTLE CHICKEN
& CHORIZO QUESADILLAS

THIS IS ONE VERSATILE DISH. ANY KIND OF TORTILLA WRAP WILL WORK A TREAT HERE: GLUTEN-FREE, WHOLEMEAL (WHOLE-WHEAT), SPINACH, SUN-DRIED TOMATO ... AND INSTEAD OF COOKING UP SOME FRESH CHICKEN, YOU CAN ALSO USE BARBECUED OR LEFTOVER COOKED CHICKEN IN THESE. SERVE WITH GUACAMOLE AND SOUR CREAM, OR THE SPICY DIPPING SAUCE FROM THE BACON-WRAPPED MINI MOZZARELLA BALLS ON PAGE 13; THE GRILLED CORN COBS FROM PAGE 49 ALSO PARTNER WELL.

SERVES 4

2 tablespoons olive oil
1 red onion, finely diced
25 g (1 oz) chorizo sausage, diced
1 garlic clove, crushed
1 yellow or orange capsicum (bell pepper), finely diced
150 g (5½ oz) chicken breast or thigh meat, finely diced
1 tablespoon hot chipotle chilli paste
2 medium-sized tomatoes, finely diced
1 teaspoon apple cider vinegar
juice of 1 lime, plus extra to serve
2 spring onions (scallions), chopped
freshly ground black pepper
2 tortilla wraps
80 g (2¾ oz) grated strong cheddar
handful of chopped coriander (cilantro) leaves

In a saucepan, heat 1 tablespoon of the olive oil over medium heat, then fry the onion, chorizo and garlic for about 10 minutes, stirring often, until the onion is soft.

Add the capsicum and chicken; you won't need any extra oil at this point, as the delicious oils from the chorizo will have oozed out. Cook for about 5 minutes, stirring so the chicken cooks all over, then stir in the chipotle sauce and the tomato. Cook for another 20 minutes or so, until the mixture is quite thick, and virtually all the moisture has cooked away.

Stir in the vinegar, lime juice and spring onion. Season with pepper and remove from the heat.

Clean out the frying pan, and heat half the remaining olive oil over medium heat. Add one of the tortilla wraps and leave for about 2 minutes, until the underside is just starting to colour. Turn it over, then scatter one-quarter of the cheddar over one half of the tortilla. Top with half the chicken mixture, one-third of the remaining cheddar and half the coriander. Cook until the cheese looks nice and melted, then fold over the bare tortilla half so you have a half-circle.

Press down with a spatula and cook for a few more minutes, then carefully flip it over and cook for another 3–4 minutes, or until crispy and brown. Remove from the pan and keep warm — or just serve it up while making the second one ...

Heat the remaining oil in the pan and repeat with the remaining tortilla wrap, cheddar, chicken mixture and coriander, to make another quesadilla.

To serve, cut each hot quesadilla in half and squeeze a little extra lime juice over the top. Serve with your choice of accompaniments.

SEAFOOD MAC 'N' CHEESE

LOBSTER MACARONI HAS BEEN AROUND FOR A WHILE NOW. IT'S HARD TO TIRE OF THAT WINNING COMBO, EVEN THOUGH IT JUST FEELS A BIT WRONG. RITZY LOBSTER, PAIRED WITH CHEAP-AS-CHIPS MACARONI? HMMM ... ANY SEAFOOD WORKS WELL THOUGH! OR WHY NOT ADD SOME BACON OR CHORIZO, OR EVEN SOME CHOPPED TOMATOES (GET RID OF THE SEEDS THOUGH). MAC 'N' CHEESE IS GREAT LIKE THAT.

SERVES 4

500 g (1 lb 2 oz) macaroni
2 tablespoons butter
3 tablespoons plain (all-purpose) flour
450 ml (15 fl oz) milk
150 g (5½ oz/1¼ cups) grated fontina
50 g (1¾ oz) grated extra-mature cheddar
1 tablespoon hot sauce
100 g (3½ oz) rocket (arugula)
300 g (10½ oz) cooked seafood, such as white crabmeat, peeled chopped prawns (shrimp), chopped lobster tails, mussels
35 g (1¼ oz) breadcrumbs, made from day-old bread
2 tablespoons grated parmesan
pinch of chilli flakes

Preheat the oven to 200°C/400°F (fan-forced).

Bring a large saucepan of salted water to the boil. Add the macaroni and cook for 8–10 minutes, or until nearly done; it should still have a little firmness. Drain well, then return to the cooking pan.

Meanwhile, melt the butter in a saucepan. Stir in the flour and cook over medium heat for about 30 seconds. Slowly add the milk in a few batches, making sure the mixture is smooth and the milk is fully incorporated before adding the next lot. Cook, stirring often, for about 5–10 minutes, until the sauce is of a fairly thick consistency. Stir in the fontina and cheddar, along with the hot sauce.

In a separate frying pan or saucepan, wilt the rocket for a minute or two over medium heat. Tip the leaves into a sieve and press with the back of a spoon to squeeze out as much liquid as you can.

Stir the cheesy sauce through the cooked and drained macaroni, along with the rocket and seafood. Transfer to a large baking dish.

Combine the breadcrumbs, parmesan and chilli flakes, and scatter over the macaroni. Bake for about 20 minutes, until golden and bubbling. Allow to cool for a minute or two, before serving with a crunchy green salad, or a rocket (arugula) salad.

EASY EMMENTAL CAULIFLOWER CHEESE SOUFFLÉS

THESE SOUFFLÉS REALLY ARE EASY, AND A NICE PLAY ON THE CLASSIC CAULIFLOWER CHEESE. JUST DON'T GO OPENING THAT OVEN DOOR UNTIL THE SOUFFLÉS ARE DONE, OR YOU AND YOUR LOVELY SOUFFLÉS WILL BE DEFLATED.

SERVES 4

1½ tablespoons butter, plus extra for greasing
1½ tablespoons plain (all-purpose) flour
320 ml (11 fl oz) milk
2 tablespoons sour cream
80 g (2¾ oz) grated emmental
60 g (2 oz/½ cup) grated cheddar
1 tablespoon wholegrain mustard
freshly ground black pepper
250 g (9 oz/2 cups) cauliflower florets
6 free-range egg whites

Melt the butter in a saucepan over medium heat. Stir in the flour and cook for about 30 seconds, then slowly add the milk. Keep stirring to make a smooth, fairly thick sauce that coats the back of the spoon, then remove from the heat and stir in the sour cream.

Return to a low heat and stir in the emmental and cheddar to make a rich, cheesy sauce. When the cheeses have melted, stir the mustard through and season with pepper. Scrape into a bowl and allow to cool to room temperature, stirring occasionally to prevent a skin forming on the surface.

While the cheese sauce is cooling, steam the cauliflower over a saucepan of simmering water for about 5 minutes, or until tender; the cooking time will depend on the size of your florets. Allow to cool slightly, then blitz to a purée and cool to room temperature. (To speed up the cooling process, you can put the cauliflower purée in a bowl and rest the base of the bowl in cold water.)

Mix the cooled cauliflower purée into the cooled cheese sauce.

Preheat the oven to 200°C/400°F (fan-forced). Generously grease two 1 litre (34 fl oz/4 cup) capacity ramekins with butter.

In a clean bowl, whisk the egg whites to stiff peaks using electric beaters. Use a metal spoon to fold the beaten egg whites into the cauliflower mixture, being careful not to knock out too much air.

Spoon the mixture into the ramekins and bake, without opening the oven, for 25 minutes, until the soufflés have puffed up and are a lovely golden brown. They should still have a very slight, gentle wobble on top.

Serve straight away!

BACON QUADRUPLE CHEESE BURGERS

A BURGER IS BASICALLY NAKED WITHOUT A LAYER OF CHEESE — SO HERE IS THE MOST FASHIONABLE, WELL-CLOTHED BURGER IN TOWN, WHERE THE PATTIES THEMSELVES ARE STUFFED WITH CHEDDAR, CLOAKED IN AMERICAN CHEESE, AND DRESSED WITH A BLUE CHEESE AND BACON SAUCE, MAKING THEM TRIPLE CHEESE, WITH THE CHEESY BUNS MAKING THEM QUADRUPLE CHEESE BURGERS ... YOU CAN ADD EVEN MORE CHEESE TO THE BURGERS IF YOU PLEASE, AND MAKE YOUR OWN CHEESY BUNS IF YOU'RE FEELING FANCY (SEE THE TIP AT THE END OF THE RECIPE). SERVE WITH A SIDE OF HOT, SALTY CHIPS.

MAKES 6

6 potato or brioche burger buns
    (or make your own; see the end
    of the recipe)
50 g (1¾ oz) grated mature cheddar
    (optional, if you're using bought
    buns)
handful of rocket (arugula) leaves
6 slices of American cheese (the
    plasticky kind where each slice
    is individually plastic-wrapped)
sliced pickles, to serve

Start by making the patties. Place the beef, egg and hot sauce in a bowl with half the cheddar, season heavily with salt and pepper and mix together with your hands. Let the mixture sit at room temperature while you get the rest of the burger extravaganza ready — but no longer than 45 minutes. (If you need to let it rest for longer, move it to the fridge, but let it come back to room temperature before you start assembling the burgers.) Mix the rest of the cheddar with the onion and set aside.

To make the blue cheese and bacon sauce, heat the olive oil in a small frying pan and fry the bacon until crispy but not burnt. Drain on paper towel, then mix in a bowl with the blue cheese, loosening the mixture with a splash of water if needed — you want it to be thick and spreadable though, so don't add too much water.

To shape and stuff the patties, divide the beef mixture into six even portions. Take one portion, divide it in half and flatten each piece in the palm of your hand, to about 1 cm (½ inch) thick, and a good burger size to fit your buns. Take a large pinch of the cheddar and onion mixture, squash it into a flattish ball, then place in the middle of one of the patty halves, leaving a clear border of at least 1.5 cm (½ inch) all the way round. Top with the other patty half, making sure your beef patty is properly sealed all around the edges. Repeat with the rest of the beef mixture and the cheddar and onion filling.

When you're ready to assemble the burgers, heat half the olive oil in a large heavy-based frying pan over high heat. Add three of the patties and fry for 3–4 minutes on each side, depending on how well you like them cooked. Rest on a plate or board while you cook the rest, adding the remaining oil to the pan.

Onion & cheddar–filled beef patties

500 g (1 lb 2 oz) lean minced (ground) beef

1 free-range egg, lightly beaten

2 teaspoons hot sauce

125 g (4½ oz/1 cup) grated mature cheddar

sea salt and freshly ground black pepper

1 small red onion, finely grated

2 tablespoons olive oil

Blue cheese & bacon sauce

1 tablespoon olive oil

6 rashers (slices) of back bacon, finely diced

120 g (4½ oz) blue cheese

If you're using bought burger buns and you'd like to top them with extra cheese, preheat the grill (broiler) while the patties are cooking and resting. Slice the buns in half and place the lids, cut side facing down, on a tray lined with foil or baking paper. Scatter with the grated cheddar and grill just until the cheese has melted and is golden brown.

Spread the blue cheese and bacon sauce over the bottom of each bun. Top with a few rocket leaves, then a beef patty. Lay a slice of American cheese on top, like a royal cloak, and finish with a couple of sliced pickles. Close the burgers with the bun lids and serve.

★ TO MAKE YOUR OWN **CHEESY BURGER BUNS**, USE THE DOUGH FROM THE MOLTEN CHEESY CHIVE DOUGH BALLS ON PAGE 17. AFTER THE DOUGH HAS RESTED FOR 1-1¼ HOURS AND HAS DOUBLED IN SIZE, KNEAD IT ON A LIGHTLY FLOURED WORK SURFACE FOR ABOUT 30 SECONDS, THEN SHAPE INTO SIX EVENLY SIZED BUNS. PLACE ON A WELL-GREASED BAKING TRAY, WITH THEIR EDGES JUST TOUCHING. COVER LOOSELY WITH PLASTIC WRAP AND LEAVE IN A WARM PLACE TO RISE FOR 30-40 MINUTES. BRUSH THE TOPS WITH 2 TABLESPOONS MILK AND SCATTER WITH 75 G (2¾ OZ) GRATED MATURE CHEDDAR. BAKE IN A PREHEATED 200°C/400°F (FAN-FORCED) OVEN FOR ABOUT 30 MINUTES, UNTIL THE BUNS ARE LIGHTLY BROWNED AND THE CHEESE IS GOLDEN.

KOREAN SPICY PORK & CABBAGE BAKE

IF YOU LOVE KIMCHI, YOU CAN USE ABOUT 200 G (7 OZ) INSTEAD OF THE CABBAGE — OR A LITTLE MORE IF YOU'RE A *VERY* KEEN FAN! PERSONALLY, I LIKE THE SWEET AND HOT FLAVOURS OF THIS SUBTLER VERSION. ENJOY WITH AN ICE-COLD BEER.

SERVES 4

2 tablespoons vegetable oil
1 onion, finely chopped
3 garlic cloves, crushed
750 g (1 lb 11 oz) lean minced (ground) pork
125 g (4½ oz) white rice
1 tablespoon chilli flakes
1–2 tablespoons gochujang (Korean red pepper paste), depending on your addiction
juice of 1 lemon
2 tablespoons honey
pinch of brown sugar or caster (superfine) sugar
400 g (14 oz) thinly sliced sweetheart or sugarloaf cabbage
sea salt and freshly ground black pepper
200 g (7 oz) mozzarella, torn
100 g (3½ oz/¾ cup) grated cheddar
3 spring onions (scallions), chopped

Heat the oil in a large saucepan or deep-sided frying pan over medium-high heat. Fry the onion and garlic for a few minutes, then stir in the pork. Cook, stirring fairly often, for about 20 minutes, until the pork is cooked through and there are some sticky brown bits. Definitely hang around for those brown bits, as they are so flavoursome, and if the pork starts to form little clumps, encourage that.

While the pork is cooking, rinse the rice in warm water, then cook according to the packet instructions, using your preferred method. Drain very well.

Preheat the oven to 180°C/350°F (fan-forced).

When the pork is cooked, reduce the heat and stir in the chilli flakes, red pepper paste, lemon juice, honey and sugar. Add the cabbage and stir-fry for 10–15 minutes, until it has wilted down and become really soft. Season with salt and pepper and give everything a good mix.

Spoon the rice into a baking dish that is about 7 cm (2¾ inches) deep, and roughly 22 cm (8¾ inches) in diameter. Top with one-quarter of the torn mozzarella, then all the pork and cabbage mixture. Scatter with the remaining mozzarella and cheddar.

Bake for 15–20 minutes, until the cheese has browned and is bubbling on top. Serve garnished with the spring onion, as the ultimate bowl-and-fork TV dinner.

GIANT FOUR-CHEESE PASTA SHELLS

WHEN THE UNIVERSE GOES HAYWIRE, AND EVERYTHING FEELS A BIT MESSED UP, YOU'LL FIND ALL THE ANSWERS YOU NEED IN A BIG CHEESY PASTA BAKE. THIS ONE'S A BIT SPECIAL BECAUSE THE PASTA IS *HUGE* AND THE CHEESE PLENTY AND VARIED — JUST LIKE LIFE'S RICH PAGEANT.

SERVES 4

16 giant pasta shells
250 g (9 oz/1 cup) ricotta
125 g (4½ oz/1¼ cups) grated
    parmesan, plus extra for the
    topping
2 mozzarella balls, roughly torn
3 tablespoons finely chopped chives
sea salt and freshly ground black
    pepper
60 g (2 oz/½ cup) grated cheddar

For the tomato sauce
1 tablespoon olive oil
1 onion, chopped
1 garlic clove, finely chopped
pinch of chilli flakes
400 g (14 oz) tin chopped tomatoes
sea salt and freshly ground black
    pepper
1 teaspoon apple cider vinegar
2 handfuls of basil leaves, torn

Start by making the tomato sauce. Heat the olive oil in a saucepan over medium heat and cook the onion and garlic for 5–10 minutes, until softened and just starting to colour. Stir in the chilli flakes, then add the tomatoes and season with salt and pepper. Bring to a gentle simmer and cook for about 20 minutes, until the sauce has thickened. Stir in the vinegar and basil leaves and remove from the heat. (If you're feeling flash, you can let it cool a little, then blitz in a blender until smooth.)

Meanwhile, cook the pasta shells in a large saucepan of salted boiling water for a few minutes less than recommended in the packet instructions. Working gently so the shells don't break, drain the pasta, rinse carefully under running cold water and leave to cool.

Preheat the oven to 200°C/400°F (fan-forced).

To make the filling, put the ricotta, parmesan and half the mozzarella in a bowl. Add the chives, season with salt and lots of pepper and mix together.

Spoon about half the tomato sauce into the base of a large baking dish, measuring about 22 cm x 30 cm (8¾ inches x 12 inches). One by one, spoon the cheesy filling into each of the pasta shells, placing them in the baking dish. When all the shells are nestled on their bed of tomato sauce, spoon the rest of the sauce over them.

Scatter the remaining mozzarella over, then the cheddar and some extra parmesan.

Bake for 25–30 minutes, or until the cheese is melted and bubbly, and some of the pasta shells have crisped up around the edges.

Serve with a simple green salad or lightly steamed broccoli.

FOUR-CHEESE BAKED PUMPKIN FONDUE

THIS FONDUE IS A REAL SHOWPIECE: A ONE-OFF RAZZAMATAZZ OF A CHEESE SENSATION. PRESENT IT IN THE MIDDLE OF THE TABLE WITH SIMPLE ACCOUTREMENTS SUCH AS SLICED APPLES, CRUSTY BREAD AND SMALL ROASTED POTATOES, AND WAIT FOR ALL THE WOWS!

SERVES 4–6

1 medium pumpkin (winter squash), weighing around 4 kg (8 lb 13 oz)
2 teaspoons freshly grated nutmeg
freshly ground black pepper
splash of olive oil
2 French shallots, finely chopped
1½ tablespoons cornflour (cornstarch)
125 ml (4 fl oz/½ cup) white wine
100 g (3½ oz/¾ cup) grated gruyère
100 g (3½ oz) grated smoked cheese
100 g (3½ oz) grated extra-mature cheddar
100 g (3½ oz) grated jarlsberg (or edam)
100 ml (3½ fl oz) thick (double/heavy) cream
1 teaspoon cayenne pepper

Preheat the oven to 180°C/350°F (fan-forced).

Using a sharp knife, carefully slice the top off your pumpkin, reserving it as a lid. Scrape out the seeds and any stringy membranes, to hollow out the pumpkin. Rub the insides with the grated nutmeg and plenty of pepper.

Place the pumpkin on a baking tray. Pop the lid back on, transfer to the oven and bake for 1 hour.

After 1 hour in the oven, continue baking the pumpkin, checking on it every 10 minutes or so, until the flesh inside is soft and comes away easily with a spoon, but the outside still holds its shape. Some pumpkins contain more moisture than others, depending on how fresh they are and where they've been stored, so cooking times will vary, and can take up to 50 minutes at this point.

When the pumpkin is nearly ready, make the fondue sauce. Heat a little olive oil in a saucepan and cook the shallot over medium heat for 3–5 minutes, or until soft. Add the cornflour and stir to coat the shallot, then add the wine. When it starts to bubble, stir in all four cheeses until they have melted, then stir in the cream. If the sauce is a bit thick, add a splash of milk, water or more wine.

Spoon the cheesy sauce into the pumpkin shell. Sprinkle with the cayenne pepper. Leaving the pumpkin lid off, return to the oven and bake for a further 20 minutes.

Serve in the middle of the table, with spoons to scrape out the softened pumpkin, covered in all that delicious melty cheese, and dipping forks on which diners can secure small chunks of bread, sliced apples or small roasted potatoes to scoop out the fondue.

CHEESE-STUFFED TURKEY MEATBALLS WITH CHEESY POLENTA

MMMM, IT'S HARD TO TELL WHICH IS THE MOST SATISFYING ELEMENT OF THIS PILE OF CHEESY GOODNESS: THE CREAMY CHEESY POLENTA, OR THE TOP-SECRET MOLTEN MOZZARELLA POCKET INSIDE THE MEATBALLS ... YOU CAN ALSO MAKE THESE MARVELLOUS MEATBALLS WITH LEAN MINCED BEEF.

SERVES 4

500 g (1 lb 2 oz) minced (ground) turkey
2 garlic cloves, crushed
1 free-range egg, beaten
4 tablespoons cooked, drained, cooled quinoa
60 g (2 oz) grated parmesan, plus extra to serve
1 tablespoon chopped thyme leaves
sea salt and freshly ground black pepper
100 g (3½ oz) block of mozzarella
2 tablespoons olive oil

First, make your meatballs. Put the turkey, garlic, egg, quinoa, parmesan and thyme in a large bowl. Season with salt and pepper and mix together using your hands.

Chop the mozzarella into 1 cm (½ inch) cubes — don't make them any larger, or the meatballs will break apart during cooking, resulting in cheese disaster.

Take a small handful of the meatball mixture and wrap it around a cube of mozzarella. Shape into a neat ball and place on a baking tray lined with baking paper. Repeat with the remaining meatball mixture and cheese cubes; you should end up with about 24 meatballs. Chill them in the fridge while you make your tomato sauce.

Preheat the oven to 200°C/400°F (fan-forced). Line another baking tray with baking paper.

To make the sauce, heat the olive oil in a saucepan and cook the onion over medium-low heat for 10 minutes, until soft, stirring often. Add the tomatoes, chilli flakes and basil, then season with salt and pepper. Leave to simmer for about 30 minutes, to thicken into a smooth sauce, then stir in the vinegar.

While your sauce is simmering, you can get on with frying the meatballs! Heat the olive oil in a large frying pan over medium–high heat. Working in several batches, so you don't overcrowd the pan, cook the meatballs for about 2-3 minutes on each side, until they are nicely browned with some crispy bits — don't remove them too soon, as you want those crispy brown bits.

Transfer the meatballs to the lined baking tray and bake for about 10 minutes, keeping an eye on them, and removing them from the oven when they are cooked through.

Tomato basil sauce

1 tablespoon olive oil

1 onion, very finely chopped

2 x 400 g (14 oz) tins chopped
tomatoes

½–1 teaspoon chilli flakes

large handful of basil leaves

sea salt and freshly ground black
pepper

1 teaspoon apple cider vinegar

Cheesy polenta

225 g (8 oz/1½ cups) instant-cook
polenta

80 g (2¾ oz) grated parmesan

30 g (1 oz/¼ cup) grated Swiss
cheese

When your tomato sauce is ready, add the meatballs and let them hang
out together over low heat while preparing the final component of this
feast: the cheesy polenta.

Cook the polenta according to the packet instructions – this usually
involves carefully whisking the polenta into a saucepan of boiling water,
then simmering for a couple of minutes; watch out for hot splatters as the
mixture bubbles up. When the polenta is cooked, stir the cheeses through.

Serve the polenta with the meatballs and tomato sauce, with an extra
parmesan snowdrift on top.

HASSELBACK CHICKEN WITH A BACON WEAVE

THIS IS A FANCIED UP VERSION OF CREAM CHEESE STUFFED IN A CHICKEN BREAST AND WRAPPED IN BACON: THE HEIGHT OF SOPHISTICATION IN THE '90S. EVERYONE LOVED IT THEN, AND EVERYONE LOVES IT NOW.

SERVES 4

120 g (4½ oz) rocket (arugula)
3 tablespoons finely chopped chives
200 g (7 oz) ricotta
1 teaspoon smoked paprika
freshly ground black pepper
4 skinless chicken breasts
80 g (2¾ oz) mozzarella
24 rashers (slices) of streaky bacon

Preheat the oven to 200°C/400°F (fan-forced). Line a baking tray with baking paper.

In a frying pan set over medium heat, wilt the rocket down with a splash of water for about 5 minutes. Remove from the heat, then mix in the chives and ricotta. Season with the paprika and lots of pepper.

Use a sharp knife to cut incisions along the length of the chicken breasts, leaving about 1 cm (½ inch) intact at the base, and spacing the incisions about 1.5 cm (½ inch) apart. Make sure you don't cut all the way through to the bottom!

Spoon the ricotta mixture into the gaps, letting some spill out onto the surface of the chicken. Tear the mozzarella and place on top of the chicken.

Now it's time to get your bacon weave on! You're going to make four bacon lattices to cover the chicken breasts. To do this, take six bacon slices. Lay three slices side by side, then the other three slices running the other way on top. Alternate overlapping the slices to make a lattice weave effect. Use your bacon lattice to loosely wrap up one of the chicken breasts, with your excellent lattice work on top, and the ends tucked underneath. Don't wrap them too tightly or the cheese will split out during cooking.

Repeat with the remaining bacon, making another three lattices to cover the remaining chicken.

Transfer to the lined baking tray and bake for 30 minutes, until the chicken is cooked through.

Serve with steamed green vegetables — or mashed potatoes if you're feeling greedy!

THREE-CHEESE BEEF LASAGNE

RATHER THAN MAKING A BÉCHAMEL SAUCE, THIS LASAGNE USES LAYERS OF UNADULTERATED CHEESE: WHY DILUTE THE CHEESE IF YOU DON'T NEED TO? FOR AN EVEN LAZIER VERSION, YOU CAN DITCH THE LASAGNE SHEETS AND HOMEMADE BEEF RAGU, AND SIMPLY LAYER THE CHEESES WITH YOUR FAVOURITE STUFFED TORTELLINI OR RAVIOLI.

SERVES 4

125 g (4½ oz) mascarpone
1 free-range egg
freshly ground black pepper
12 lasagne sheets, approximately
handful of basil leaves
150 g (5½ oz) mozzarella, torn
40 g (1½ oz) grated parmesan

Beef ragu
1 tablespoon olive oil
1 onion, finely chopped
1 garlic clove, crushed
pinch of chilli flakes
500 g (1 lb 2 oz) minced (ground) beef
1 tablespoon tomato paste (concentrated purée)
2 x 400 g (14 oz) tins chopped tomatoes
sea salt and freshly ground black pepper
1 tablespoon thyme leaves
handful of basil leaves
1 teaspoon apple cider vinegar or lemon juice

Start by making the ragu. Heat the olive oil in a saucepan and fry the onion and garlic over medium heat for about 8 minutes, stirring often, until the onion is starting to soften. Stir in the chilli flakes, then the beef. Cook for about 10 minutes, stirring regularly so the beef browns lightly all over; let some bits turn crispy and brown, as this will make it extra tasty.

Stir in the tomato paste, then the chopped tomatoes. Season with salt and pepper, add the thyme leaves and tear in the basil leaves. Leave to simmer for about 20 minutes, until you have a thick ragu. Stir the vinegar through.

Meanwhile, preheat the oven to 180°C/350°F (fan-forced). In a bowl, beat the mascarpone with the egg and season with pepper.

Find yourself a baking dish, about 6 cm (2½ inches) deep, and measuring about 18 cm x 23 cm (7 inches x 9 inches). Spoon a 1 cm (½ inch) layer of the ragu over the base of the dish.

Top with a layer of lasagne sheets — break pieces off some sheets if they don't fit neatly in the dish. Spread half the mascarpone mixture over the sheets, then cover with half the mozzarella. Scatter over some basil leaves and season with lots of pepper.

Cover with more lasagne sheets, then spoon half the remaining ragu over. Top with more lasagne sheets and the rest of the mascarpone mixture and mozzarella. Season with more pepper and scatter with the remaining basil.

Cover with a final layer of lasagne sheets and the rest of the ragu. Sprinkle with the grated parmesan.

Cover with foil, then bake for 25 minutes. Remove the foil and bake for a further 15–20 minutes, until the sauce is bubbling around the edges and the cheese is melted and browned on top.

Leave to sit for about 5 minutes, before serving with a crunchy green salad or some rocket (arugula) leaves — and maybe some garlic bread if you're feeling greedy ...

CHEESE
SWEETS

CHEDDAR ICE CREAM

IF YOU'RE FEELING TOTALLY OUT OF CONTROL, YOU CAN SERVE THIS ALREADY OVER-THE-TOP ICE CREAM WITH LITTLE BITS OF STICKY CANDIED BACON ON TOP.

MAKES ENOUGH FOR 10 SERVINGS

6 free-range egg yolks
200 g (7 oz) caster (superfine) sugar
pinch of sea salt
350 ml (12 fl oz) full-fat milk
250 ml (8½ fl oz/1 cup) thick (double/heavy) cream
1 vanilla bean, split lengthways, seeds scraped
150 g (5½ oz) mature cheddar, grated
popping candy, to serve

In a large bowl, whisk together the egg yolks, sugar and salt until pale and creamy. Set aside.

In a heavy-based saucepan, gently heat the milk and cream. When the mixture is just starting to steam — don't let it boil! — remove from the heat to cool slightly, then gradually whisk it into the beaten egg yolks.

Return the mixture to the saucepan over low heat. Add the vanilla pod and seeds and keep stirring until the mixture thickens to a custard consistency — it should easily coat the back of the spoon and stay there.

Remove from the heat, discard the vanilla pod, then stir in the cheddar until melted.

Transfer to a bowl and leave to cool down completely, then chill in the fridge, before churning and freezing in an ice cream maker according to the manufacturer's instructions.

The ice cream will keep in the freezer for a month or two.

Serve with popping candy on top.

★ IF YOU DON'T HAVE AN ICE CREAM MAKER, FREEZE THE CHILLED CUSTARD MIXTURE IN A LARGE SHALLOW CAKE TIN FOR 2-3 HOURS, OR UNTIL JUST FROZEN AROUND THE EDGES. WHISK TO DISTRIBUTE THE ICE CRYSTALS THROUGH THE MIXTURE. REPEAT EVERY HOUR, SEVERAL TIMES, UNTIL YOU HAVE AN ICE CREAM WITH A SMOOTH, EVEN TEXTURE.

PEANUT BUTTER CHEESECAKE POTS WITH PEANUT BRITTLE

A DECONSTRUCTED CHEESECAKE WITH EXTRA PEANUTY CRUNCH. WHO KNEW PEANUTS AND CHEESE WERE SUCH GREAT DESSERT BUDDIES?

MAKES 6

180 g (6½ oz) full-fat cream cheese
200 g (7 oz) ricotta
80 ml (2½ fl oz/⅓ cup) thick (double/heavy) cream
60 g (2 oz/½ cup) icing (confectioners') sugar
75 g (2¾ oz) smooth peanut butter
2 tablespoons finely ground peanuts

Peanut biscuit base
100 g (3½ oz) peanut-laced biscuits (cookies)
45 g (1½ oz/⅓ cup) crushed peanuts
50 g (1¾ oz) butter, melted

Peanut brittle
butter, for greasing
120 g (4½ oz) caster (superfine) sugar
1 teaspoon sea salt
80 g (2¾ oz/½ cup) crushed peanuts
1 teaspoon vanilla extract

Make the base by whizzing up the biscuits and peanuts in a food processor into chunky crumbs — or place them in a sealed bag and whack them with something heavy. Mix the crumbs with the melted butter.

You'll need six 'pots' with fairly wide mouths and deepish sides for these little treats; fat tumbler glasses, about 300 ml (10 fl oz) capacity, are a good choice. Press the crumb mixture loosely into the bottom of your pots. Chill in the fridge to firm up while preparing the other elements of these greedy little puddings.

In a bowl, whip the cream cheese, ricotta, cream and icing sugar with a fork or spoon until thick and fluffy. Fold in the peanut butter and ground peanuts; they don't have to be completely incorporated — a few ripples look great. Spoon the mixture onto the biscuit bases and chill in the fridge for 1 hour, or even overnight if you're making them ahead.

Meanwhile, make the peanut brittle. Grease a baking tray with butter, and scatter over half the peanuts. Put the sugar in a small, spotlessly clean saucepan over medium–low heat. Leave it alone to dissolve completely, giving it a very gentle swirl every so often to loosen any lumps; try not to stir it too much. You should end up with a molten mass of caramel-coloured sticky syrup. Add the salt and vanilla extract, give a quick stir, and then immediately pour the mixture onto the buttered baking tray, then scatter over the other half of the peanuts. Leave it to set and harden, at room temperature, for about 10 minutes. (Don't put it in the fridge, or you may need a trip to the dentist when you try to eat it!)

When it has set, break the brittle into six neat shards, and crush some of the broken-off chunks to a rough powder. (You may have some larger pieces left over, but it isn't very practical to make brittle in smaller quantities, so save these bits for snacking, or to add some flair to other desserts. Keep in an airtight container at room temperature until you need them.) About 10 minutes before serving, remove the chilled cheesecakes from the fridge to bring them to room temperature. Decorate with the peanut brittle shards and ground peanut brittle and tuck in.

LEMONY CREAM CHEESE DONUTS

TOTALLY OUTRAGEOUS AND UNBELIEVABLY DELICIOUS. THESE ARE ACTUALLY REALLY EASY. DON'T BE A DONUTS. JUST MAKE THEM.

MAKES 12–14

2 teaspoons fast-acting dried yeast
1 tablespoon caster (superfine) sugar, plus extra for dusting
40 g (1½ oz) butter
220 ml (7½ fl oz) milk
1 free-range egg
500 g (1 lb 2 oz/3⅓ cups) plain (all-purpose) flour, plus extra for dusting
2 tablespoons soft brown sugar, plus extra for dusting
1 teaspoon sea salt
vegetable oil for deep-frying

Combine the yeast with 125 ml (4 fl oz/½ cup) warm water and a pinch of the caster sugar. Give it a swirl and leave it alone for 10 minutes somewhere warm, until the yeast starts to foam.

Meanwhile, in a small saucepan, melt the butter with the milk; remove from the heat and leave to cool. Whisk in the egg.

Put the remaining caster sugar in a large bowl, along with the flour, brown sugar and salt. Slowly add the milk mixture, working it into the dry ingredients with your hand. Mix in the yeast mixture, until you have a soft dough that is not too dry and not too sticky; sprinkle in a little more flour if it's very sticky, or a splash more milk if it's a little dry. Cover with plastic wrap and leave for 10 minutes.

Turn the dough out onto a lightly floured work surface and start to knead it. Keep kneading for 10 minutes, until the dough has a firmer consistency. Put the dough back in the bowl, cover with plastic wrap and leave in a warm place for 1¾ hours, until doubled in size.

On a freshly floured worktop, very briefly knead the dough. Let it rest for a few minutes, then shape it into a rough rectangle about 2 cm (¾ inch) thick — don't use a rolling pin for this, as it can be too heavy handed.

Use a 7 cm (2¾ inch) cutter to cut out 12 circles, rerolling any scraps (but no more than twice). Lightly shape them so they are a little rounder, then place on lightly floured baking trays with plenty of space between them. Cover with plastic wrap and leave to rise somewhere warm for another 30 minutes to puff up again.

Scatter a thickish layer of extra caster sugar and brown sugar into a shallow bowl or deep plate, ready to roll the donuts in.

Lemon mascarpone filling
zest of 1 lemon
250 g (9 oz) mascarpone
2 teaspoons lemon curd
2 teaspoons poppy seeds

In a deep saucepan measuring about 20 cm (8 inches) across, heat about 10 cm (4 inches) of vegetable oil over medium-high heat to 185°C (365°F), or until a small piece of bread dropped in fizzes and turns brown within 30 seconds. Keep an eye on the oil temperature so it doesn't get too high or drop too low; check the temperature using a kitchen thermometer, if you have one — if the oil's not hot enough, the donuts won't cook properly and may be soggy!

Carefully lower in the donuts, no more than two or three at a time. Cook for 2-3 minutes, turning them over frequently so they brown evenly. Carefully lift them out using tongs or a slotted spoon, roll them in the sugar mixture, then place on another plate or tray to cool.

Mix together all the filling ingredients. Spoon into a piping (icing) bag fitted with a nozzle.

When the donuts have cooled to room temperature, make a little hole in one side and pipe in the filling — you may have some filling left over, depending on how much your donuts have puffed up.

The donuts are best enjoyed the same day they are made.

★ INSTEAD OF DUSTING THE DONUTS WITH SUGAR AND FILLING THEM WITH THE LEMON MASCARPONE, YOU COULD GLAZE THE PLAIN DONUTS WITH A **LEMON & POPPY SEED GLAZE**. COMBINE 200 G (7 OZ) ICING (CONFECTIONERS') SUGAR WITH THE JUICE OF 1 LEMON AND 1 TEASPOON POPPY SEEDS. SLATHER THE GLAZE OVER THE COOLED DONUTS.

GOAT'S CHEESE & MAPLE SYRUP NECTARINE TARTS

MORNING, NOON OR NIGHT, HERE'S A SOPHISTICATED WAY TO SATISFY THOSE SWEET CHEESE URGES. DON'T USE REALLY RIPE NECTARINES THAT ARE OOZING JUICE, OR THEY WILL COLLAPSE IN THE OVEN — SAVOUR THOSE ONES AS NATURE INTENDED. IF NECTARINES AREN'T IN SEASON, APPLES ARE AN ADMIRABLE SUBSTITUTE.

MAKES 6

plain (all-purpose) flour, for dusting
1 sheet of frozen ready-rolled puff pastry, thawed
6 tablespoons soft spreadable goat's cheese
1 tablespoon chopped thyme leaves
4–5 nectarines (or apples), stones removed, flesh sliced into 1 cm (½ inch) wedges
6 teaspoons maple syrup
6 teaspoons raw (demerara) sugar

Preheat the oven to 200°C/400°F (fan-forced). Place a baking tray in there to heat up.

On a lightly floured work surface, cut the pastry down the middle lengthways, and then twice widthways, to give you six even pieces. Prick the pastry all over with a fork, and separate the pieces out a little bit.

Mix the goat's cheese with half the thyme leaves. Spread 1 tablespoon of the mixture over each piece of pastry, leaving a 1 cm (½ inch) border all around each edge.

Arrange the nectarine slices on top (about three quarters of a nectarine per piece of pastry). Drizzle each tart with 1 teaspoon maple syrup, then sprinkle with 1 teaspoon sugar. Sprinkle with the remaining thyme.

Cook in the oven for about 15 minutes, or until the pastry is golden and puffed.

Serve warm, with cream if desired.

CHEESECAKE FREAKSHAKE

THE SECRET TO THIS EXTRAVAGANZA OF A MILKSHAKE IS TO MAKE IT SO THICK IT HOLDS UP ALL THE CREAM AND TOPPINGS. IF THINGS START COLLAPSING, JUST SCOOP IT ALL UP WITH A SPOON. YOU WILL NEED A GOOD LIE DOWN AFTER THIS ONE.

MAKES 2

strawberry sauce (the stuff in a squeezy bottle that you pour over ice cream)
freeze-dried strawberries or raspberries
hundreds and thousands
3 large scoops of strawberry ice cream
3 large scoops of vanilla ice cream
200 g (7 oz) frozen strawberries
200 g (7 oz) New York cheesecake
100–150 ml (3½–5 fl oz) full-fat milk
squirty cream
mini marshmallows or other sweets, to decorate
crushed pistachio nuts, optional

Dip two 500 ml (17 fl oz/2 cup) mason jars in strawberry sauce, to coat the rim by about 3 cm (1¼ inches) all the way round. Crumble some freeze-dried berries, mix them with some hundreds and thousands, and use this mixture to coat the rim.

Put all the ice cream in a blender with the frozen strawberries. Break 120 g (4¼ oz) of the cheesecake into chunks and add to the blender, along with 100 ml (3½ fl oz) of the milk and 1 tablespoon of the strawberry sauce. Whiz gently to combine into a thick shake, adding more milk if it needs loosening.

Pour the milkshake into your jars. Squirt some cream in a neat spiral on top. Cut the remaining cheesecake into 1–1.5 cm (½ inch) cubes and arrange on top of the cream — don't make them too big or the milkshake may collapse in on itself.

Decorate with sweets, crushed pistachios, more hundreds and thousands and freeze-dried berries, in an over-the-top manner.

Finish with a final flourish of strawberry sauce and serve with a straw, or a spoon, or both.

HEAVENLY FLOURLESS ALMOND RICOTTA CAKE

THIS RICH, TORTE–LIKE CAKE MAKES AN ENVIABLE DESSERT. EVEN BETTER, YOU CAN MAKE IT A DAY AHEAD, AS THE TEXTURES AND TASTES WILL ONLY IMPROVE OVERNIGHT IN THE FRIDGE. LET IT SIT AT ROOM TEMPERATURE FOR 15 MINUTES BEFORE SERVING WITH A SCOOP OF CRÈME FRAÎCHE.

MAKES ONE 22 CM (8¾ INCH) CAKE

butter, for greasing
225 g (8 oz) dark chocolate, broken into evenly sized pieces
1½ teaspoons ground cardamom seeds
450 g (1 lb) ricotta
4 free-range eggs, separated
zest of 1 orange
juice of 2 oranges
275 g (9½ oz) caster (superfine) sugar
275 g (9½ oz) almond meal

Dreamy mascarpone icing
225 g (8 oz) mascarpone
1 tablespoon orange juice
165 g (6 oz/1⅓ cups) icing (confectioners') sugar
3 tablespoons good-quality unsweetened cocoa powder
orange zest, to garnish

Preheat the oven to 180°C/350°F (fan-forced). Grease a 22 cm (8¾ inch) springform cake tin.

Find a heatproof bowl large enough to hold all the cake batter ingredients. Add the chocolate bits and place the bowl over a saucepan of just simmering water, taking care that the bottom of the bowl doesn't touch the hot water. Stir the chocolate occasionally so it melts evenly; when it has melted, remove from the heat.

Stir in the cardamom, then mix in the ricotta, egg yolks, orange zest and juice, sugar and almond meal.

In a clean bowl, using electric beaters, whisk the egg whites until just before stiff peaks start to form. Being careful not to lose too much air, gently fold the beaten egg whites through the chocolate mixture; you want the mixture to be streak-free.

Scrape the batter into the cake tin and smooth the surface. Bake for 50 minutes to 1 hour, until a skewer inserted into the middle of the cake comes out mostly clean — a few sticky bits are good, as this is meant to be a very moist cake.

Remove from the oven and leave to cool in the tin for a few minutes, before turning out onto a wire rack to cool completely.

To make the icing, beat the mascarpone and orange juice together in a bowl using a wooden spoon, then beat in the icing sugar and cocoa powder until thick and creamy.

When the cake has cooled completely, slather the icing over the top and garnish with some grated orange zest. On a hot day, you may want to chill the cake for a few minutes, just to firm up the icing before slicing.

This cake will keep in an airtight container in the fridge for several days.

CHEESE-CRUST APPLE CHEDDAR PIE

USING A MIX OF SPELT FLOUR AND PLAIN FLOUR GIVES THE PASTRY A NUTTY FLAVOUR AND WHOLESOME TEXTURE IN THIS TRADITIONAL OLDE ENGLISH CHEESE AND APPLE PIE. ONCE IT'S OUT OF THE OVEN, SOME GREEDY PEOPLE EVEN SERVE THE PIE WITH A SLICE OF CHEESE *ON TOP*.

SERVES 4

1.5 kg (3 lb 5 oz) apples; granny smiths work well
100 g (3½ oz) raw (demerara) sugar
1 free-range egg, beaten
150 g (5½ oz) mature cheddar, sliced

Find yourself a round pie dish about 7 cm (2¾ inches) deep and 24 cm (9½ inches) wide.

Now make the cheesy pastry for your magnificent pie. In a large bowl, combine the flours, sugar and nutmeg, then rub in the butter until the mixture looks like breadcrumbs. Mix in half the grated cheddar, reserving the rest of the cheddar for sprinkling over the finished pie. Add the milk, a tablespoon at a time, and work it in to form a dough. If there are bits of dry pastry in the bottom of the bowl, add more of the milk, but try not to let the dough get sticky.

Cut off one-third of the dough and set it aside for the pastry lattice.

On a lightly floured work surface, roll out the larger piece of dough to about 5 mm (¼ inch) thick. Carefully lift it over the pie dish (using the rolling pin to help carry it over) and lower it in. Gently press the dough all around the bottom edge of the dish and up the sides, leaving at least 4 cm (1½ inches) of pastry overhanging the rim, for the lattice lid to attach to. Trim away any excess overhanging pastry.

Roll out the smaller bit of pastry to a rectangle 5 mm (¼ inch) thick, and a little larger than the top of the pie dish. Cut into strips 2 cm (¾ inch) wide. Lay the strips on a baking tray lined with baking paper.

Chill all the pastry in the fridge for 45 minutes.

Meanwhile, preheat the oven to 180°C/350°F (fan-forced) and place a baking tray in there to heat up.

Without piercing all the way through the pastry, prick the chilled pie base several times with a fork. Loosely line it with scrunched-up baking paper and fill with baking beads, dried beans or rice.

Cheddar pastry

200 g (7 oz/1⅓ cups) plain (all-purpose) flour, plus extra for dusting

200 g (7 oz/1¾ cups) spelt flour

2 tablespoons caster (superfine) sugar

1 teaspoon freshly grated nutmeg

200 g (7 oz) salted butter, chilled and diced

200 g (7 oz) grated mature cheddar

60 ml (2 fl oz/¼ cup) milk, plus a splash extra if needed

Place the pie dish on the hot tray in the oven and blind bake for about 15 minutes, until the pastry is lightly golden. Remove the paper and beads and cook for a further 5 minutes, until the pastry feels dry to the touch; it shouldn't be too dark brown though.

Remove the pie dish from the oven, but leave the baking tray in there. Allow the pastry shell to cool right back down to room temperature.

While the pastry is blind baking, prepare the filling. Peel and core the apples and slice about 5 mm (¼ inch) thick. Pat the slices dry, then place in a colander. Scatter the sugar over and toss to coat, then leave to drain for 30 minutes. The apples will release their liquid, which will help avoid a soggy pie. Pat dry with paper towel.

Lightly brush the cooled pastry base with some of the beaten egg. Arrange a layer of apple slices in the bottom of the pie. Add a layer of cheddar slices, then alternate more slices of apple and cheddar, finishing with a layer of cheese.

Make a lattice pattern with the pastry strips. Brush the pastry rim with beaten egg, then lay the lattice lid over the filling and press onto the pastry rim to seal. Trim off the overhang, then use your fingers to pinch the pastry together all the way around the edge, to seal and make a pretty crust.

Brush the lattice strips with more beaten egg. Scatter over the reserved grated cheddar and bake for 40 minutes, until the pastry is golden and delicious and the cheese has browned.

Leave to cool for 10 minutes, before serving with chutney ice cream. Only joking: serve with cream or regular ice cream — or perhaps the Cheddar ice cream on page 94.

This pie is best served warm, but will keep in an airtight container in the fridge for a day or two.

EASY SANDWICH BISCUITS

THIS IS A REALLY LAZY CHEAT'S RECIPE. YOU CAN, OF COURSE, MAKE YOUR OWN COOKIES, BUT WHY WOULD YOU BOTHER WHEN YOU CAN BUY THEM?

MAKES 12

24 biscuits (cookies) of your choice, such as Viennese whirls; they can be as plain or fancy-looking as you like

Classic filling
100 g (3½ oz) mascarpone
210 g (7½ oz/1¾ cups) icing (confectioners') sugar
pinch of sea salt

Choc vanilla variation
1 teaspoon vanilla extract
1 tablespoon good-quality unsweetened cocoa powder

The extravagant variation
1 tablespoon popping candy
1 tablespoon hundreds and thousands, plus extra to decorate

Hot pink variation
1 teaspoon vanilla extract
all-natural pink food colouring

Make a batch of the classic filling by beating the mascarpone in a bowl with the icing sugar and salt using a wooden spoon. You can now just sandwich your biscuits together with this easy cheesy delight of a filling — or make one or all of the filling variations below.

To make all three variations, divide the basic filling mixture among three bowls. Into one bowl, fold the vanilla extract and cocoa powder.

Into another portion, fold the popping candy and hundreds and thousands.

Into the final portion, fold the vanilla extract and a tiny amount of food colouring to turn it your desired pink.

Use a knife to spread the filling on the flat side of 12 biscuits, then sandwich the remaining biscuits on top, flat side down.

Roll the 4 extravagant biscuits in the extra hundreds and thousands, for a bit of extra colour.

And biscuits that aren't devoured straight away will keep in an airtight container in the fridge for several days; bring them to room temperature for serving.

CHOCOLATE ORANGE CHEESECAKE

THIS IS LIKE A GIANT CHOCOLATE ORANGE, BUT IN CAKE FORM, AND WITH CHEESE. I THINK ALL YOUR PRAYERS MAY HAVE BEEN ANSWERED IN ONE DAY.

MAKES ONE 22 CM (8¾ INCH) CAKE

150 g (5½ oz) butter

300 g (10½ oz) packet of digestive biscuits, preferably chocolate-orange flavour, but you can use plain ones, or other solid-type biscuits (cookies)

Choc orange topping

150 g (5½ oz) orange chocolate (or a mix of regular chocolate and orange chocolate), broken into evenly sized pieces

1 teaspoon orange liqueur (optional)

560 g (1 lb 4 oz/2¼ cups) full-fat cream cheese

150 g (5½ oz) icing (confectioners') sugar

1 tablespoon fine unsweetened cocoa powder

200 ml (7 fl oz) thick (double/heavy) cream, well chilled

40 g (1¼ oz) edible confetti sprinkles, preferably gold (optional)

Melt the butter in a small saucepan, then remove from the heat and leave to cool.

Break the biscuits roughly into a food processor and whiz to make crumbs, or place them in a sealed bag and whack them with something heavy. Tip them into a bowl, then give it a shake; if you see any larger crumbs, break them up. Mix in the cooled butter.

Pack the buttery crumbs into the base of a 22 cm (8¾ inch) springform cake tin. Make sure the layer is perfectly even and level, without hilly biscuit regions, to give you that desired perfectly straight base edge when you slice the cheesecake. Think Holland, not Switzerland. Chill in the fridge while you get on with the topping.

Melt most of the chocolate (reserving some for decorating) in a heatproof bowl set over a saucepan of gently simmering water — do not let the bottom of the bowl touch the hot water. Stir gently to help the chocolate melt evenly. Stir in the orange liqueur, if using, then leave to cool a little bit.

In a bowl, beat the cream cheese, icing sugar and cocoa powder together with a wooden spoon until smooth and creamy. Beat in the cooled melted chocolate until smooth and creamy again.

Using an electric whisk, beat the cream into soft peaks, then fold it through the chocolate mixture, keeping it all lovely and light, but trying to get rid of any streaks. Then, fold the confetti sprinkles through if using.

Scrape the choc orange topping onto the chilled biscuit base. Chill in the fridge for about 8 hours, or until firm — just in time for breakfast ...

The cheesecake will keep in an airtight container in the fridge for a day or two. Serve straight from the fridge, decorated with the reserved chocolate.

WARM CHEESE PIE WITH APRICOT & PISTACHIOS

CHEESE PIE? YES PLEASE! ANY RICH, CREAMY, RIND CHEESE (SUCH AS CAMEMBERT OR BRIE) WILL WORK LIKE A DREAM HERE. AND USE A THICK JAM ON TOP — ONE THAT IS ALMOST OF A CHUTNEY CONSISTENCY, RATHER THAN THE RUNNY KIND.

SERVES 2–4

plain (all-purpose) flour, for dusting
1 sheet of frozen ready-rolled puff pastry, thawed
250 g (9 oz) round of camembert
2–3 tablespoons thick apricot or fig jam (or cranberry jelly for a festive flavour)
1 tablespoon crushed pistachio nuts
milk, for brushing

Preheat the oven to 220°C/430°F (fan-forced) and get a baking tray in there to heat up.

Dust a sheet of baking paper or foil with flour and place the pastry sheet on top. Place the round of camembert in the middle, then spread the jam over. Top with the crushed pistachios.

Wrap the pastry loosely around the cheese. Don't stretch it or pull it too tight around the base, as this can lead to molten cheese leaking out in the oven — disaster! Twist off the excess pastry at the top. Brush the pastry lightly with milk, and poke a few holes in the top to let out any steam during baking.

Transfer to a sheet of baking paper, then place on the hot tray in the oven. Bake for 20 minutes, or until the pastry is puffed and golden.

Leave to cool for a few minutes, before presenting the warm pie to your dinner party (or just to yourself). Serve warm.

INDEX

Smith Street Books

Published in 2017 by Smith Street Books
Melbourne | Australia
smithstreetbooks.com

ISBN: 978-1-925418-31-6

CIP data is available from the National Library of Australia

Publisher: Paul McNally
Editor: Katri Hilden
Concept Design: Billy Law
Design Layout: Heather Menzies
Photographer & Stylist: Billy Law

Printed & bound in China by
    C&C Offset Printing Co., Ltd.
Book 30
10 9 8 7 6 5 4 3 2 1

THANK YOU!

A huge thank you to everyone who has helped put together this beautiful dedication to the wonder that is cheese.

To Paul McNally at Smith Street Books for being as excited about the idea of a whole book celebrating CHEESE as me! And for generally being great. To Billy Law and Heather Menzies for the excellent design, and also to Billy for the gorgeous photos that show off cheese in all its glory. And to Katri Hilden for keeping it in check editorially.

A massive thank you to my loyal and patient cheese testers: my sister, Ruth, my mum and dad, and to my amazing extended family, Lara, Jay, Jack and Shubox, Mark, Evelyn and Arthur, Carole and Mervyn. Also a very grateful thank you to Sharon (at 9 months pregnant, she showed true cheese dedication; I'm so relieved that the cake still scored enough points with Chris, even when it was scraped off the floor), and also to Amy and Louise for stepping up to the cheese plate. Amazing to have so many cheese fans in my life!

Also, to my husband Andy who took up running with me during the testing of these recipes. We ate an obscene amount of cheese … those were some good times …

And of course to you the reader for loving cheese as much as me. #cheeselove